Tactics for **Boosting** Academic Achievement

70 Ways to Increase Student Success

Gale Naquin, Ph.D. and Tammy Stephens, M.Ed.

Sopris West™
EDUCATIONAL SERVICES

A Cambium Learning Company

BOSTON, MA • LONGMONT, CO

Printed in the United States of America

Published and Distributed by

Sopris West™
EDUCATIONAL SERVICES

A Cambium Learning Company

4093 Specialty Place • Longmont, CO 80504 • 303-651-2829

www.sopriswest.com

112395/236/9-06

Dedication

To my husband and daughter—
> *thank you for your love and support.*

Ronnie, Connie, and Lis—
> *thanks for believing in me.*

Grandma—
> *all kids need a brilliant teacher; **you** have been mine.*

—Tammy

To my three children, Clint, Ryan, and Jaclyn—
> *thanks for being the miracles of my life.*

To the teachers and children—
> *who have inspired me to make this book possible*

—Gale

About the Authors

Gale Naquin, **Ph.D.**, is currently the grant director of the Prereferral Assessment Model at the University of New Orleans (UNO). She has spent the past nine years developing and refining the model with her colleagues from UNO and Louisiana State University. She also teaches graduate courses in assessment at UNO and Southeastern Louisiana University. Naquin received her doctorate in educational administration with a minor in special education. She has 30 years of educational experience as a classroom teacher, an administrator at the  state and local levels in both the public and private education sectors, an educational diagnostician, and a university professor.

For years, Naquin has served as an active officer in the Council for Exceptional Children (CEC). She is a past president of the Council of Educational Diagnostic Services (CEDS) and of the Louisiana Federation of CEC. She is currently the president of the Teacher Education Division of CEC for the Louisiana Division.

Naquin is an author of the book *Teaching Effective Classroom Routines*. She is working with colleagues to prepare new teacher institutes and professional development schools. Her research interests and expertise include assessment techniques, teacher efficacy, organizational reform of the referral process, and service delivery for students who are at risk. Naquin has presented more than 200 papers at national and local conferences, and she has served as a consultant for public and private school districts' advocacy groups and for mental health providers.

Tammy Stephens, **M. Ed.**, is an educational diagnostician in Keller, Texas. She has three years of teaching experience working with students who display emotional, behavioral, and learning problems. She earned a bachelor's degree in human services counseling from Old Dominion University and a master's degree in education (emphasis on special education) from the University of New Orleans. Stephens completed assessment coursework at Texas Woman's University  for certification as an educational diagnostician. She is completing coursework at Texas Woman's University and the University of North Texas, working toward a doctorate in special education.

Stephens has experience working with students who have emotional and behavioral disorders, dyslexia, learning disabilities, and autism. Her research interests include finding comprehensive and effective teaching strategies to use with all learning styles, early intervention strategies, researching and implementing effective behavior management techniques, and finding effective social skills programs to use with students having emotional and behavioral disorders.

Contents

Chapter One: Reading Tactics—In Chapter One, nearly all tactics are appropriate for all students, those with and those without learning disabilities. The exceptions are "Improving Comprehension Using ASK IT" and "Improving Comprehension Using TRAVEL," both of which are designed specifically for students who have learning disabilities.

Chapter Two: Spelling Tactics—In Chapter Two, nearly all tactics are appropriate for all students, those with and those without learning disabilities. The exception is "Improving Skills Using Word–Sentence–Word Format," which is designed specifically for students who with low-functioning spelling ability. **109**

Chapter Two: Tactic name	Age/grade level	Page
Improving Skills Using Letter Tiles	Elementary	111
Improving Skills Using Scrambled Words	Elementary through secondary	114
Improving Skills Using Read and Draw	Early elementary through secondary	117
Improving Skills Using Glitter Writing	Early elementary through secondary	119
Improving Skills Using Sandpaper Cut Outs	Early elementary	121
Improving Skills Using Alphabet Stamps	Early elementary	123
Improving Skills Using Newspaper Cut Outs	Early elementary	125
Improving Skills Using Sand Writing	Early elementary	127
Improving Skills Using Word Searches	Early elementary	129
Improving Skills Using Link Letters	Early elementary	132
Improving Skills Using Modified Cloze	Early elementary	134
Improving Skills Using Word–Sentence–Word Format	Third grade	137
Improving Skills Using Making Words	Elementary and secondary	139
Improving Skills Using Word Walls	Elementary and secondary	143
Improving Skills Using Add a Word	Elementary and secondary	145
Improving Skills Using the Write–Say Method	Elementary	147

Introduction

If the student hasn't learned, the teacher hasn't taught.
—Siegfried Engelmann

Tactics for Boosting Academic Achievement is a practical sourcebook presenting 70 academic tactics that have been empirically demonstrated to improve academic achievement. The book integrates recent research in the field of academic problems and tactics into a single reference, containing academic tactics in each of the basic skills: reading, language arts (including spelling), and mathematics.

All of the tactics in this book are designed for easy implementation by all teachers. Each tactic is delineated in a brief format that describes the time it takes to deliver the tactic session, the tactic objective, needed materials, and preparation considerations. Additionally, each tactic provides a Coach Card that provides step-by-step implementation procedures. Reproducible checklists, student worksheets, and data recording sheets for keeping track of student progress are provided. Included with several tactics are samples of completed worksheets, sample reading passages, and reading probes.

Tactics for Boosting Academic Achievement uses a direct-instruction approach to increase the probability that teachers can and will use effective academic strategies and students will correctly master them. This approach includes three stages—tell, show, and do:

1. *Tell*: Students are *told* how to use the skill or strategy.

2. *Show*: Students are *shown* how to use the strategy by role playing and modeling.

3. *Do*: Students *do* the skill by practicing the skill with teacher supervision.

The tactics are built on the notion that the teacher frequently praises the student, offers corrective feedback, and systematically monitors the tactic.

Tactics for Boosting Academic Achievement is particularly useful for general classroom teachers, special education teachers, school psychologists, educational diagnosticians, consultants, and intervention assistance teams. This book can also be used as a key reference for teacher practitioner programs when training is being provided to those who are new to the field of education. The tactics in this book are designed to meet the needs of students in various learning environments. Each tactic can be used with students in the general education classroom who struggle with a concept or who need extra practice, as well as with students who receive services in a special education classroom.

These tactics are a great way to reinforce concepts learned and to check for understanding after a concept is taught. Teachers can use each tactic to gather pertinent information regarding their students' current level and progress. For example, by implementing a tactic to all students in the classroom, the teacher can determine whether to move forward to a new tactic or to review a tactic that previously has been taught.

It is very important for teachers to follow these guidelines (Fulk & King, 2001):

1. Explain the purpose and rationale for the technique. When explaining the reasons for using peer tutoring, stress the idea of increased opportunities for practice and "on-task" behavior.

2. When discussing the use of peer tutoring, place emphasis on collaboration and cooperation rather than competition.

3. Select and provide the needed materials for tactic implementation prior to the practice session.

4. Train the students in the roles of tutor and tutee. Review specific procedures to be used with (a) feedback for corrective responses, (b) error correction, and (c) recording scores on data recording sheets.

5. Model appropriate behaviors for the tutor and tutee. Be sure to demonstrate acceptable ways to give and accept corrective feedback.

6. Provide the written tactic for student practice of roles, and allow time for practice and rehearsal.

7. Allow opportunities for tutors and tutees to practice roles as the teacher circulates, providing feedback and reinforcement.

8. Conduct further discussions regarding constructive and nonconstructive pair behaviors. Answer questions and problem solve as needed.

9. Repeat Step 8.

Research shows there are many benefits to using peer tutors in the classroom. Ehly (1986) suggests peer tutoring programs can improve the academic skills of tutors as well as tutees. According to Garcia-Vazquez & Ehly (1995), peer tutoring programs improve the social skills of both the tutor and tutee. Studies have also found peer tutoring to be beneficial when used with students with learning disabilities, emotional and behavioral disabilities, and mild mental retardation, as well as students at risk for academic failure or those with limited English proficiency (Fulk & King, 2001).

It is important for the teacher to remember that tutors are not teachers—they do not teach new skills. Instead, peer tutors are ideal for the role of "helper," to motivate and encourage students who are struggling in an academic area. Before assigning students to be tutors, teachers need to ensure that the students have mastered the necessary essential skills.

Teachers should also conduct periodic "tutoring integrity checks." Adults who supervise peer tutors should occasionally drop in to observe tutoring sessions. These checks can make the supervisor aware of tutors who might be lapsing from the prescribed tutoring format and might need additional training to improve tutoring skills. All of the tactics found in this book can be implemented through the help of a teacher, teacher's aide, or peer helper.

Tutors and tutees can be selected and paired in several different ways. Some researchers suggest that teachers should randomly select and pair students, whereas others say that teachers should pair students after pretesting student skill levels. A systematic method for pairing is to rank students by achievement (high to low), divide the list of names in two, and pair the first student in List 1 with the first student in List 2 (Fulk & King, 2001). Although all of these strategies are effective ways of pairing tutors with tutees, teachers should make educated decisions as to which method best works for their classroom.

Providing appropriate training for the tutor and tutee is a very important part of the implementation process. Students respond more appropriately when they are provided with a rationale and a purpose for using the peer tutoring strategy. Place emphasis on collaboration rather than competition (i.e., "When we help one another, everyone wins"), and emphasize that the purpose is to help each other learn.

Another important part of the training is modeling and discussing appropriate ways to provide corrective feedback. Various combinations may be used during the training process (i.e., two adults, teacher and student, or two students). Teachers may use short skits to demonstrate appropriate and inappropriate responses and social behaviors. Role playing with prepared scripts is another effective method of demonstrating positive ways for peers to interact with one another. The goal of this process is to prevent students from becoming aggressive or demeaning toward their partners.

Finally, to ensure successful use of the peer tutoring program, it is important to demonstrate the role of the tutor. Teachers should teach the tutors how to ask questions and deliver content appropriately and should demonstrate appropriate delivery of positive feedback and correction (see the following example).

Sample script for providing positive feedback:

Following a correct response, the tutor says, "Yes, that's right."

Following an incorrect response, the tutor says, "Nice try, but the correct answer [or word] is _____. Now you say it. Good job!"

To provide frequent reinforcement, after every third response the tutor should say, "Good job! You're really working hard today."

1

Reading Tactics

The man who can make hard things easy is the educator.

—Ralph Waldo Emerson

Introduction

Good readers are able to comprehend what they read by following cognitive processes before reading, during reading, and after reading. Because they are strategic, metacognitive, and motivated when reading, good readers are more likely to be able to generalize and maintain their reading skills than those readers who lack acquisition, fluency, and metacognition skills.

Research supports major instructional approaches for developing comprehension skills (National Reading Panel, 2000; Adams & Englemann, 1996). Such approaches include reciprocal teaching, direct instruction, and transitional strategies instruction. The reading tactics in this chapter incorporate all three instructional approaches.

The first approach, *reciprocal teaching*, takes place in the form of a dialogue between the teacher and student. This instructional strategy involves teaching students four comprehension strategies: predicting, questioning, seeking clarification, and summarizing. In reciprocal teaching, students work together, taking turns as "teacher."

The second approach, *direct instruction*, involves teacher explanation and modeling of effective strategies, followed by opportunities for students to practice the strategies during reading. Teacher explanation and modeling decrease as students become more independent in strategy use.

The third approach, *transitional strategies instruction*, is characterized by direct explanation and modeling; that is, teachers provide additional instruction (e.g., mini-lessons) as students practice strategies and model and explain the use of strategies for one another. Additionally, students are provided with information about the usefulness of strategies and when and where to use them as teachers model the use of strategies for students throughout the day.

The tactics found in this chapter can be used with narrative or expository texts. This chapter begins with a tactic involving large-word decoding skills and a tactic covering word recognition skills. In order to become effective readers, students must be able to use phonological strategies to dissect and sound out words (Good, Simmons, & Smith, 1998). Students must be able to manipulate the sounds produced by each letter in the word in order to read the word. Having the ability to sound out the word and recognize words by sight in a fluent manner increases reading comprehension.

Next in the chapter are tactics that increase reading fluency. Fluent readers are able to read orally with speed, accuracy, and proper expression. Fluency is one of several critical factors necessary for reading comprehension (National Reading Panel, 2000). Fluent readers have better reading comprehension skills than those who laboriously read over each word, having to break down and sound out each letter. Such arduous reading results in a loss of meaning. Student progress may be monitored using the same Data Recording Sheet.

Finally, the remainder of the chapter is dedicated to tactics that help the student comprehend the material being read. Using various strategies, students increase their reading comprehension and become active participants in the learning process. Tactics presented in this chapter teach students to think about the topic prior to beginning to read, pulling in prior knowledge and allowing students to link the reading material to experiences they have had with the topic. The tactics also provide students with strategies that encourage them to examine the layouts of textbooks (the ways in which material is presented), giving each student a better understanding of the material. Ultimately, many of the tactics presented teach students ways to organize the material being read in a way that makes it more manageable and understandable.

Several tactics in this chapter may involve using coaches to help coach students through the decoding word and reading comprehension processes. There is more to reading than just recognizing and reading words. Students must be able to apply meaning to the words being read in order to maintain good reading comprehension. The tactics in this chapter provide students with techniques that will help improve their reading comprehension and allow active learning.

Matching Uppercase and Lowercase Letters

Objective: This tactic is designed to increase the student's ability to identify and form uppercase and lowercase letters.

Materials: Daily folder, Uppercase and Lowercase Letter Charts, Uppercase and Lowercase Letter Cards, Scrambled Uppercase and Lowercase Letters Sheets 1 and 2, scissors, timer, and Data Recording Sheet.

Preparation: Make copies of tactic reproducibles and gather remaining tactic materials. Cut out the letter cards.

 Requires approximately **10–15 minutes** each day (two to three times per week).

Coach Card

- ❑ Get materials and go to an assigned work area. Cut one page of letters into squares to make cards.

- ❑ **Model**: Begin by using half the alphabet. Using your pointer finger, trace a letter on the chart while saying its name aloud. Write the same letter in the air.

- ❑ **Model**: Given two letter cards, point to and say the letter being worked on (choose one of the two letter cards). Repeat this procedure for five letters. Refer to the letter chart for assistance. The teacher may randomly choose two letters from the pile of 13 and work on one letter at a time for a total of five letters, or the teacher may specify the letters to address depending on the student's needs.

- ❑ **Guided practice**: Instruct the student to trace the letter with his/her finger.

- ❑ Instruct the student to write letter in the air.

- ❑ Give the student two letter cards. Have the student identify the letter being worked on out of the two choices. The student may refer to the letter chart if needed. Repeat this process until all letters are practiced.

- ❑ **Assessment**: Take out the Scrambled Letters Sheet 1. Set timer for three minutes. Point to a letter on the page and instruct the student to say its name. Repeat this procedure for the 13 letters being worked on. The 13 letters being worked on may be the same as those on the scrambled sheet, or they may be random depending on the student's needs. When these letters have been mastered, begin with the second half of the alphabet.

- ❑ When timer buzzes, stop working.

- ❑ Record score on Data Recording Sheet.

Matching Uppercase and Lowercase Letters:
Uppercase Letter Chart

A	B	C
D	E	F
G	H	I
J	K	L
M	N	O
P	Q	R
S	T	U
V	W	X
Y	Z	

Matching Uppercase and Lowercase Letters:
Lowercase Letter Chart

a	b	c
d	e	f
g	h	i
j	k	l
m	n	o
p	q	r
s	t	u
v	w	x
y	z	

Matching Uppercase and Lowercase Letters:
Uppercase Letter Cards

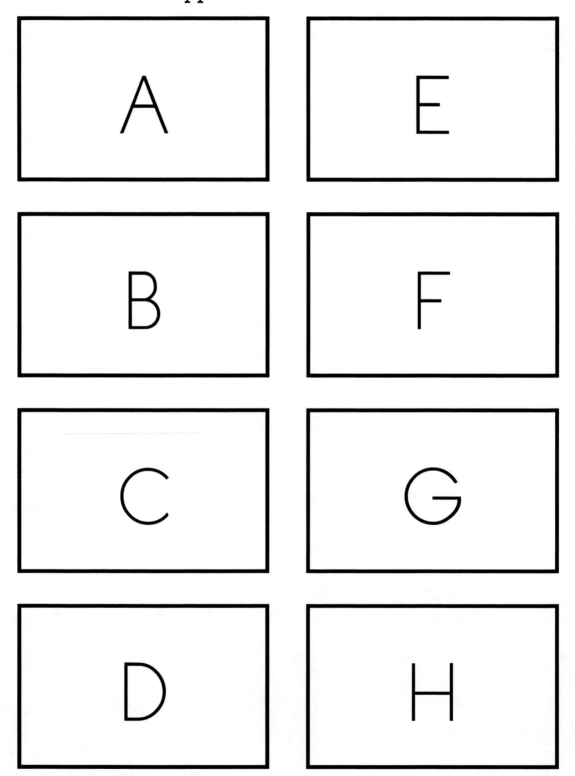

Chapter 1 • *Tactics for Boosting Academic Achievement*   Matching Uppercase and Lowercase Letters

Matching Uppercase and Lowercase Letters:
Uppercase Letter Cards

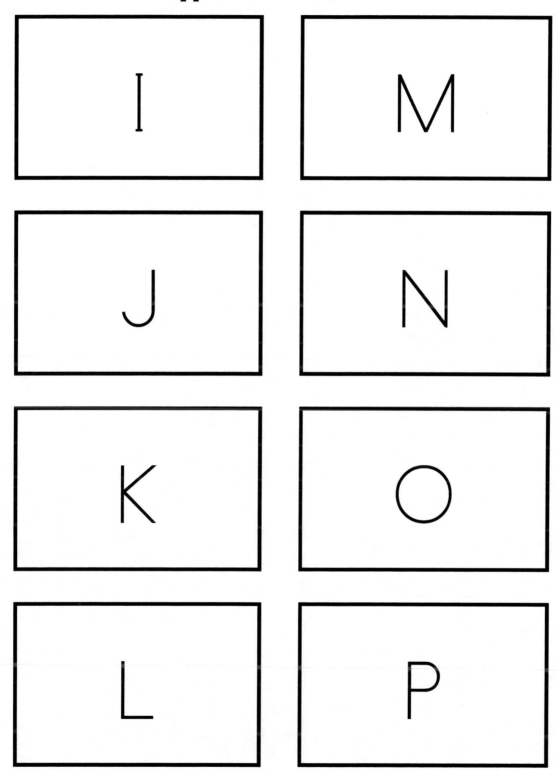

Matching Uppercase and Lowercase Letters:
Uppercase Letter Cards

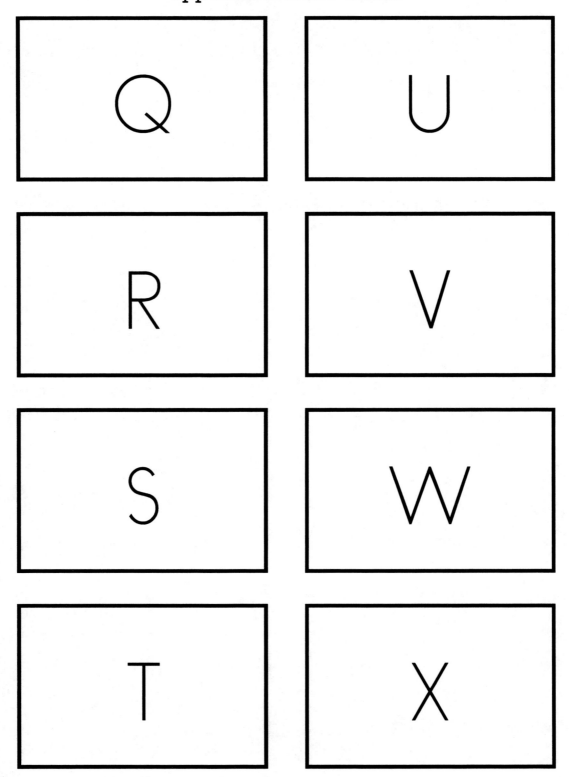

Matching Uppercase and Lowercase Letters:
Uppercase Letter Cards

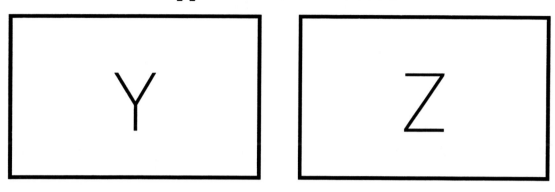

Matching Uppercase and Lowercase Letters:
Lowercase Letter Cards

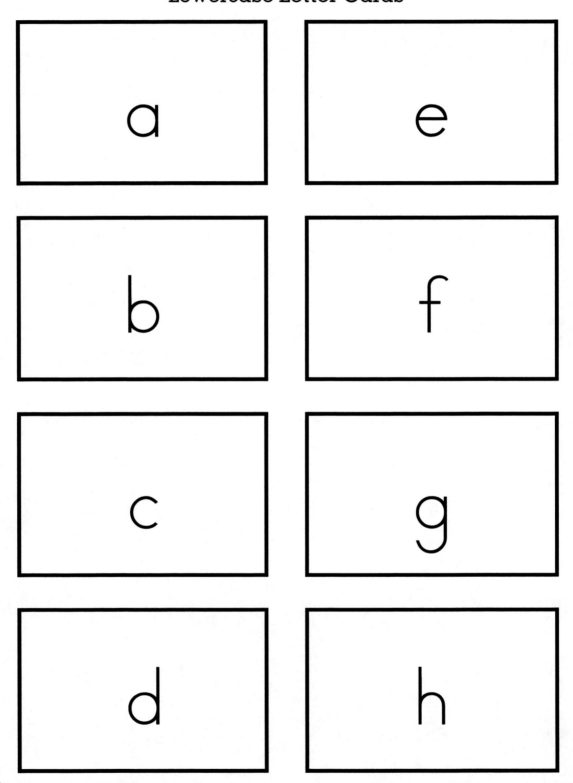

Chapter 1 • *Tactics for Boosting Academic Achievement*   Matching Uppercase and Lowercase Letters

Matching Uppercase and Lowercase Letters:
Lowercase Letter Cards

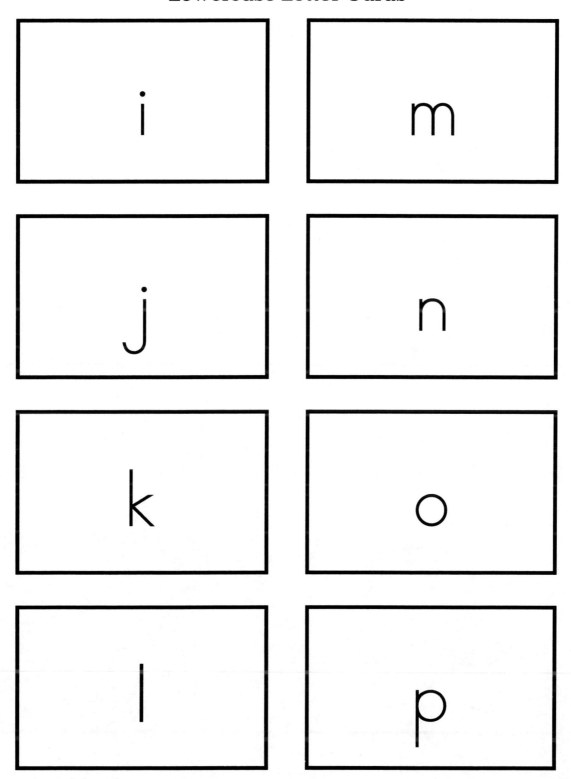

Matching Uppercase and Lowercase Letters:
Lowercase Letter Cards

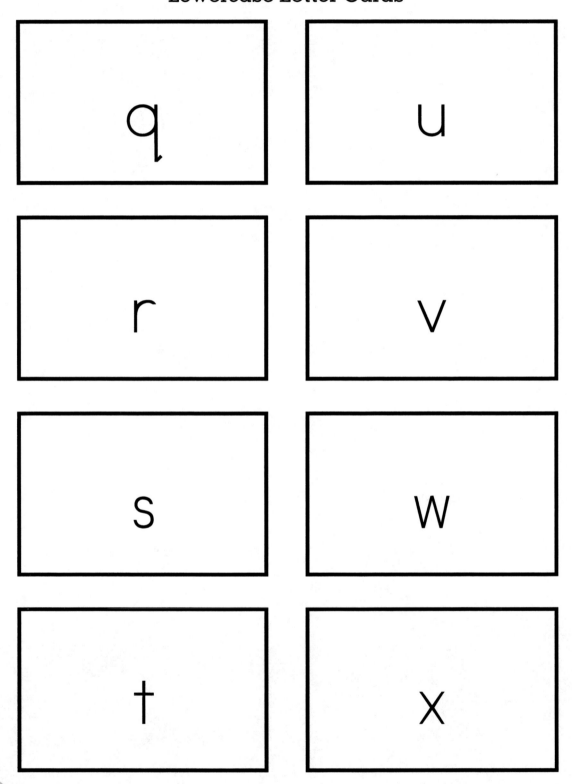

q

u

r

v

s

w

t

x

Matching Uppercase and Lowercase Letters:
Lowercase Letter Cards

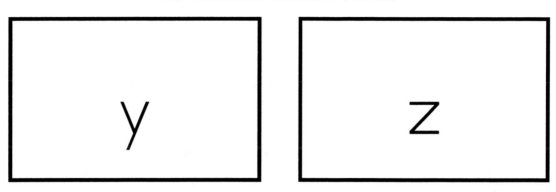

Matching Uppercase and Lowercase Letters:
Scrambled Uppercase Letters, Sheet 1

H   E   G

B   M   C

K   A   L

D   J   F

I

Matching Uppercase and Lowercase Letters:
Scrambled Uppercase Letters, Sheet 2

T	U	P
Q	Y	O
N	X	S
Z	W	R
V		

Matching Uppercase and Lowercase Letters:
Scrambled Lowercase Letters, Sheet 1

e   c   b

i   a   g

h   m   l

f   d   j

k

Matching Uppercase and Lowercase Letters:
Scrambled Lowercase Letters, Sheet 2

p   r   y

u   z   n

o   x   q

w   s   v

t

Matching Uppercase and Lowercase Letters: Data Recording Sheet

Student: _____ Grade: _____

Teacher: _____ Date begun: _____ Date ended: _____

| Date | Uppercase Letters | | | | Lowercase Letters | | | |
| | Number of letters | | | Letters needing more practice | Number of letters | | | Letters needing more practice |
	Attempted	Identified correctly	Identified incorrectly		Attempted	Identified correctly	Identified incorrectly	

Notes:

Using Guide Words to Alphabetize

Objective: This tactic is designed to build fluency and increase accuracy when using dictionary guide words.

Requires approximately **15 minutes** each day (two times per week).

Materials: Daily folder, Alphabetical Order Worksheet, weekly spelling word list, timer, pencil, and Data Recording Sheet.

Preparation: Gather tactic materials. Make two copies of the Alphabetical Order Worksheet with identical spelling word lists, and one copy with a similar spelling word list to be used for assessment. Make copies of remaining tactic reproducibles and gather remaining materials.

Teacher Design: Teachers may use the Alphabetical Order Worksheet (see Sample Alphabetical Order Worksheet) provided or use the template to create a worksheet that meets the needs of his/her students.

Coach Card

- ❑ Get materials. Go to an assigned practice place. Find the day's Sample Alphabetical Order Worksheet.

- ❑ **Coach**: Show the student where the spelling word on the right fits in the alphabetical list of guide words on the left. Do this for each word in the spelling word list, writing the word on the appropriate blank line.

- ❑ **Guided practice**: Instruct the student to use another copy of the same worksheet to go through the same procedure. Encourage the student to use the alphabetical list of guide words, found directly below the worksheet directions, to determine if the spelling word fits before or after the guide word.

- ❑ The student should mark the line before or after the guide word to show his/her understanding of where the spelling word falls alphabetically in reference to the guide word.

- ❑ **Assessment**: Set the timer for one minute. Present the student with a worksheet with a similar spelling word list. Have the student alphabetize as many words as possible without assistance for the one-minute period. Student will complete the worksheet by marking the line before or after the guide word. When the timer buzzes, ask the student to stop.

- ❑ **Coach**: Record results on the Data Recording Sheet.

23

Using Guide Words to Alphabetize:
Sample Alphabetical Order Worksheet

Student: Andy   Grade: 3

Teacher: Ms. Larson   Date: March 5

Directions: Alphabetize the words from the spelling word list by writing them in the appropriate sections between the guide words.

Guide Words:	Spelling word list:
art	art
ask	
Atlantic	enough
	Atlantic
blister	
bossy	farmer
carnival	
	bossy
drifter	
elegant	elegant
elephant	carnival
enough	
farmer	

© Sopris West Educational Services. This page may be photocopied.

Using Guide Words to Alphabetize:
Alphabetical Order Worksheet

Student: _____ Grade: _____

Teacher: _____ Date: _____

Directions: Alphabetize the words from the spelling word list by writing them in the appropriate sections between the guide words.

Guide Words:	**Spelling word list:**
art	
	_____
blister	
	_____
forward	
	_____
house	_____
	_____
morning	
	_____
sister	_____
	_____

Using Guide Words to Alphabetize:
Data Recording Sheet

Student: _____   Grade: _____

Teacher: _____   Date begun:_____

                                                  Date ended:_____

Date	Number of words ordered correctly	Number of words ordered incorrectly	Total number of words ordered

Notes:

Decoding Words Using DISSECT

Objective: As a result of this tactic, the student will be able to decode words while reading.

Materials: Daily folder, paper, pencil, grade-appropriate reading material from student textbooks or other grade-appropriate reading passages, Worksheet, timer, Data Recording Sheet, and dictionary.

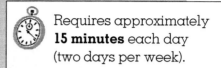
Requires approximately **15 minutes** each day (two days per week).

Preparation: Make copies of tactic reproducibles and gather tactic materials. Choose grade-appropriate reading material (see Sample Reading Passage) to be used during this tactic.

Teacher design: Teachers may choose reading passages from student textbooks, download reading passages, use Skill Builder reading passages, or create reading passages.

Coaching Checklist

☐ Get materials and go to an assigned work area. Write names, grade, and date on the Worksheet.

☐ Have student read the provided Sample Reading Passage, or other passage, aloud. When the reader comes upon a word he/she doesn't know, complete the following steps:

☐ **Model: D**—DISCOVER the context. (1) While reading, write any words you do not know on the Worksheet. (2) While reading, skip the difficult word and then use sentence clues to guess the word. (If the reader does not pronounce the word correctly, continue through the next step.)

☐ **Model: I**—ISOLATE the prefix and attempt to pronounce the word.

☐ **Model: S**—SEPARATE the suffix and attempt to pronounce the word.

☐ **Model: S**—SAY the stem of the word. (If the student cannot say the stem, proceed to the next step.)

☐ **Model: E**—EXAMINE the word. (1) If the stem begins with a vowel, pronounce units of two letters. (2) If the stem begins with a consonant, separate and pronounce units of three letters. (If the student has completed these five steps and still does not know the word, continue to the next step.)

☐ **Model: C**—CHECK. Ask the coach or teacher to help you pronounce the word.

☐ **Model: T**—TRY. Look the word up in the dictionary.

☐ **Assessment**: Present the student with a reading passage (Skill Builder reading passage). Set the timer for one minute. Have the student read as many words as possible using the steps reviewed. Evaluate reading using the Data Recording Sheet. When the timer buzzes, stop.

☐ **Coach**: Write the score on the Data Recording Sheet.

Decoding Words Using DISSECT: Worksheet

Student: _____ Grade: _____

Teacher: _____ Date: _____

𝔻 —**DISCOVER** the context. Write words you do not know from the reading passage.

_____

_____

_____

𝕀 —**ISOLATE** the prefix and attempt to pronounce the word.

_____

_____

𝕊 —**SEPARATE** the suffix and attempt to pronounce the word.

_____

_____

𝕊 —**SAY** the stem of the word.

_____

_____

𝔼 —**EXAMINE** the word. If the stem begins with a vowel, pronounce units of two letters. If the stem begins with a consonant, separate and pronounce units of three letters.

_____

_____

ℂ —**CHECK**. Ask the coach to help you pronounce the word.

𝕋 —**TRY**. Look the word up in the dictionary.

_____

_____

Decoding Words Using DISSECT: Sample Reading Passage

Plants make their own food by using water, carbon dioxide, chlorophyll, and sunlight. The process by which plants make food is called photosynthesis. Photo means "light" and *synthesis* means, "putting." In photosynthesis, plants put together materials to make food with the energy of the sunlight.

Photosynthesis takes place mainly in a plant's leaves. Certain cells in the leaf have most of the leaf's chloroplasts. These structures contain chlorophyll, the pigment that gives plants their green color.

Flesch-Kincaid Grade Level: 7.1

Decoding Words Using DISSECT: Worksheet

Student: _Brandon_   Grade: _5_

Teacher: _Ms. Sanders_   Date: _October 6_

D —DISCOVER the context. Write words you do not know from the reading passage.

Photosynthesis

I —ISOLATE the prefix and attempt to pronounce the word.

Photo synthesis

S —SEPARATE the suffix and attempt to pronounce the word.

Photo synthes is

S —SAY the stem of the word.

Photo synthes is

E —EXAMINE the word. If the stem begins with a vowel, pronounce units of two letters. If the stem begins with a consonant, separate and pronounce units of three letters.

syn the sis

C —CHECK. Ask the coach to help you pronounce the word.

T —TRY. Look the word up in the dictionary.

Decoding Words Using DISSECT:
Data Recording Sheet

Student: _____

Grade: _____

Teacher: _____

Date begun:_____

Date ended:_____

Date	Number of words read correctly	Number of errors

Notes:

Recognizing High-Frequency Words

Objective: This tactic is designed to build fluency in reading high-frequency words and monitor progress using reading passages.

 Requires approximately **5 minutes** each day (three days per week).

Materials: Daily folder, high-frequency word list (spelling list or Dolch Sight Words), two copies of the reading probe to be used during the assessment portion (i.e., Skill Builders or other reading passage controlled to reflect student's instructional level as determined by informal or formal assessments), timer, pencil, and Data Recording Sheet.

Preparation: Make copies of tactic reproducibles and gather remaining tactic materials. Prepare copies of reading probe and high-frequency word list.

Coaching Checklist

❑ Get materials and go to an assigned work area. Take out the high-frequency word list.

❑ Read all the words aloud to the student.

❑ Now have the student read the words aloud with you.

❑ Have the student read the words independently while you provide help (i.e., immediately correct mistakes, prompt correct answers, and give the student the word after a three-second hesitation).

❑ Mark the words that you help the student to read correctly.

❑ Take out the two copies of the reading passage and give one to the student.

❑ **Assessment**: Set the timer for one minute. Have the student read aloud independently for one minute while you follow along on a separate copy of the same passage. As the student reads, mark errors (i.e., skipped words, mispronounced words, and words told to the student after the three-second hesitation). When the timer buzzes, ask the student to stop reading. Draw a vertical line (|) after the last word read. Count the number of words read correctly and the number of errors, and write these numbers at the top of the page.

❑ **Coach**: Record these numbers on the Data Recording Sheet.

Chapter 1 • *Tactics for Boosting Academic Achievement*

Recognizing High-Frequency Words

Recognizing High-Frequency Words: Dolch Sight Words

This is a list of high-frequency words that readers should know immediately. The first part of the list is alphabetical.

a	cold	grow	may	said	too
about	come	had	me	saw	try
after	could	has	much	say	two
again	cut	have	must	see	under
all	did	he	my	seven	up
always	do	help	myself	shall	upon
am	does	her	never	she	us
an	done	here	new	show	use
and	don't	him	no	sing	very
any	down	his	not	sit	walk
are	draw	hold	now	six	want
around	drink	hot	of	sleep	warm
as	eat	how	off	small	was
ask	eight	hurt	old	so	wash
at	every	I	on	some	we
ate	fall	if	once	soon	well
away	far	in	one	start	went
be	fast	into	only	stop	were
because	find	is	open	take	what
been	first	it	or	tell	when
before	five	its	our	ten	where
best	fly	jump	out	thank	which
better	for	just	over	that	white
big	found	keep	own	the	who
black	four	kind	pick	their	why
blue	from	know	play	them	will
both	full	laugh	please	then	wish
bring	funny	let	pretty	there	with
brown	gave	light	pull	these	work
but	get	like	put	they	would
buy	give	little	ran	think	write
by	go	live	read	this	yellow
call	goes	long	red	those	yes
came	going	look	ride	three	you
can	good	made	right	to	your
carry	got	make	round	today	
clean	green	many	run	together	

*Edward W. Dolch, "Basic Sight Vocabulary." *Elementary School Journal*. 36, March 1936, pp. 456–460. Published by The University of Chicago Press, Copyright 1936 by The University of Chicago. All rights reserved.

Recognizing High-Frequency Words:
Data Recording Sheet

Student: _____   Grade: _____

Teacher: _____   Date begun:_____

Date ended:_____

Date	Number of words read correctly	Number of errors

Notes:

Chapter 1 • *Tactics for Boosting Academic Achievement*   Recognizing High-Frequency Words

Fluency Building for First and Second Grade Students

Objective: This tactic is designed to build fluency and increase accuracy in reading.

Materials: Daily folder, two copies of a reading passage controlled to reflect the student's instructional level (teacher should determine through use of formal/informal assessments and/or student work; see Sample Reading Passage for ideas), timer, pencil, and Data Recording Sheet.

Preparation: Make copies of tactic reproducibles and gather remaining tactic materials.

 Requires approximately **7 minutes** each day (two to three days per week).

Coach Card

- ❑ Get materials and go to an assigned work area. Take out the student's copy of the reading passage.

- ❑ **Model**: Read the passage aloud to the student.

- ❑ **Guided practice**: Have the student read the passage aloud to you. Instruct the student to use his/her pointer finger to follow the words as he/she reads. If the student gets stuck on a word for three seconds, tell the student the word. Prompt the student to pronounce the words correctly and immediately correct mistakes.

- ❑ **Assessment**: Set the timer for one minute. Have the student read aloud independently for one minute while you follow along on a separate copy of the same passage. Mark errors (skipped words, mispronounced words, and words told to the student after the three-second hesitation) as the student reads. When the timer rings, ask the student to stop reading and draw a vertical line (|) after the last word read. Count the number of words read correctly and the number of errors. Write these numbers at the top of the page.

- ❑ **Coach**: Write these numbers on the Data Recording Sheet.

Fluency Building for First and Second Grade Students: Sample Reading Passage

Instructions: Say each word.

The girl saw the sun rise early in the ~~morning~~.	(10)
The sun was bright and yellow. The birds	(18)
were singing loudly outside her window. Meg	(25)
looked outside and saw a blue | bird sitting	(33)
in a nest. The nest was high in the tree.	(43)

Flesch Reading Ease: 99.8
Flesch-Kincaid Grade Level: 0.9

Errors	Number of words read	Number of words read correctly
1	31	30

Fluency Building for First and Second Grade Students: Data Recording Sheet

Student: _____   Grade: _____

Teacher: _____   Date: _____

Date	Number of words read correctly	Number of errors

Notes:

Fluency Building for Third Through Sixth Grade Students

Objective: This tactic is designed to build fluency and increase accuracy in reading.

Materials: Daily folder, two copies of a reading passage of 200–300 words controlled to reflect instructional-level words, timer, pencil, and Data Recording Sheet.

Preparation: Make copies of tactic reproducibles and gather remaining tactic materials. Prepare copies of instructional-level reading passages.

 Requires approximately **7 minutes** each day (two to three days per week).

Coach Card

☐ Get materials and go to an assigned work area. Take out the student's copy of the reading passage.

☐ **Model**: Read the first 100 words of the passage aloud to the student. Read more slowly than you normally would and point to the words as you read.

☐ **Guided practice**: Have the student read the first 100 words of the passage aloud to you. Instruct the student to use his/her pointer finger to follow the words as he/she reads. If the student gets stuck on a word for three seconds, tell the student the word. Prompt the student to pronounce words correctly and immediately correct mistakes.

☐ **Assessment**: Take out your copy of the reading passage for scoring. Set the timer for one minute. Have the student read aloud independently for one minute while you follow along on a separate copy of the same passage. Mark errors (skipped words, mispronounced words, and words told to the student after the three-second hesitation) as the student reads. When the timer rings, draw a vertical line (|) after the last word read. Count the number of words read correctly and the number of errors. Write these numbers at the top of the page.

☐ **Coach**: Record these numbers on the Data Recording Sheet.

Fluency Building for Third Through Sixth Grade Students: Data Recording Sheet

Student: _____   Grade: _____

Teacher: _____   Date: _____

Date	Number of words read correctly	Number of errors

Notes:

Paraphrasing Using RAP

Objective: This tactic is designed to help students recall main ideas and facts from reading materials.

Materials: Daily folder, paper, pencil, grade-appropriate reading material (i.e., choose a text passage), Worksheet, timer, dictionary, and Data Recording Sheet.

Preparation: Make copies of tactic reproducibles and gather remaining tactic materials. Make copies of grade-appropriate reading material.

 Requires approximately **15 minutes** each day (two to three days per week).

Coach Card

☐ Get materials and go to an assigned work area. Write names, grade, and date on the Worksheet.

☐ **Model: R**—READ a paragraph silently, paying close attention to word meaning.

☐ **Model: A**—ASK: (1) Identify and write the main idea of the paragraph. (2) Identify and write the main details of the paragraph.

☐ **Model: P**—PUT: (1) Write the main idea of the passage in your own words. (2) Write the major details in your own words.

☐ **Assessment**: Ask the student to summarize the main idea and major details of the passage by writing a short summary.

☐ **Coach**: Evaluate the summary and write the score on the Data Recording Sheet.

Paraphrasing Using RAP: Worksheet

Student: _____   Grade: _____

Teacher: _____   Date: _____

R—READ the paragraph silently. Pay close attention to word meaning.

A—ASK

(1) Identify and write the main idea of the paragraph:

_____

_____

_____

(2) Identify and write the main details of the paragraph:

_____

_____

_____

P—PUT

(1) Write the main idea of the passage in your own words:

_____

_____

_____

(2) Write the major details of the passage in your own words:

_____

_____

_____

Paraphrasing Using RAP: Data Recording Sheet

Student: _____ Grade: _____

Teacher: _____ Date: _____

RAP components	Possible points	Points earned
R—READ	5	
A—ASK	5	
P—PUT	5	
Total	**15**	

Notes:

Building Vocabulary
Using Semantic Mapping

Objective: This tactic is designed to help students make connections between new vocabulary and prior knowledge and to see the relationships among conceptual ideas.

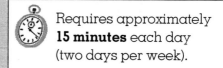
Requires approximately **15 minutes** each day (two days per week).

Materials: Daily folder, grade-appropriate expository reading material, timer, paper, Semantic Map Graphic Organizer (see Sample Semantic Map Graphic Organizer), pencil, *and two Data Recording Sheets as described on the Coach Card.*

Preparation: Make copies of tactic reproducibles and gather remaining tactic materials. Select grade-appropriate expository reading material (i.e., science or social studies) and make copies. Prior to implementation, choose chapter vocabulary word(s) that the student needs help with or does not know well.

Coach Card

- ❑ Get materials and go to an assigned work area. Find the day's worksheet containing the vocabulary word. Write names, grade, and date on the Semantic Map Graphic Organizer.

- ❑ Instruct students to read the Sample Reading Passage or other appropriate passage silently.

- ❑ Instruct students to identify the main topic and place it at the center of the Semantic Map Graphic Organizer.

- ❑ Brainstorm words that are associated with the main topic.

- ❑ Think about how to group these words into broad categories and discuss the meanings of the words.

- ❑ Identify four major categories to extend from the main idea.

- ❑ Provide labels for the categories and write them in shapes extending from the main idea.

- ❑ Generate two to eight subcategories per category and write them in shapes that are linked to the category shapes.

- ❑ **Coach**: Review and score worksheet. Write student scores on the Worksheet Data Recording Sheet at the end of this tactic.

- ❑ **Assessment**: Set the timer for one minute. The student should read the passage aloud to the teacher. Instruct the student to stop when the timer buzzes. Instruct the student to tell the teacher what the passage was about, again setting the timer for one minute. Using the Data Recording Sheet (Assessment Component) found at the back of this chapter, the teacher should mark the number of words from the passage that the student uses during the retell.

- ❑ **Coach**: Record the number of words used during the retell on the Assessment Data Recording Sheet.

Building Vocabulary Using Semantic Mapping:
Sample Semantic Map Graphic Organizer

Student: _____   Grade: _____

Teacher: _____   Date: _____

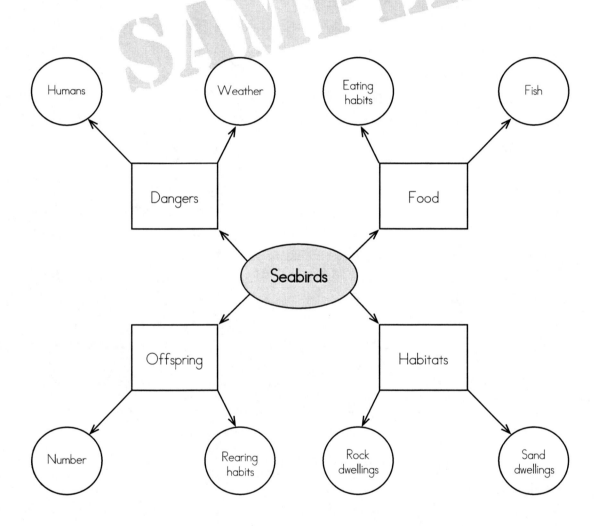

Chapter 1 • *Tactics for Boosting Academic Achievement*   Building Vocabulary Using Semantic Mapping

Building Vocabulary Using Semantic Mapping:
Semantic Map Graphic Organizer

Student: _____   Grade: _____

Teacher: _____   Date: _____

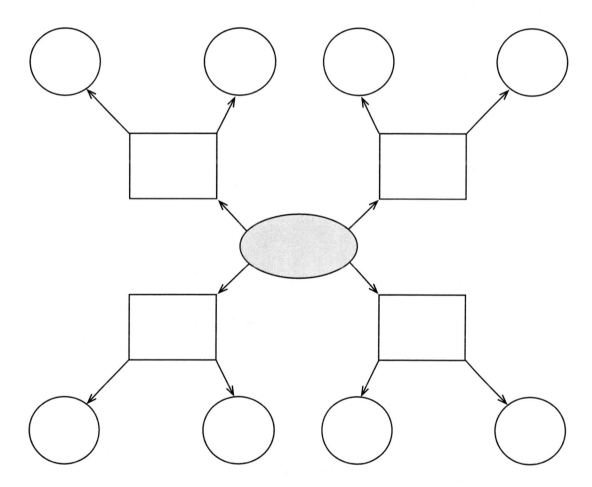

Building Vocabulary Using Semantic Mapping:
Sample Reading Passage

Instructions: Say each word.

The girl saw the sun rise early in the morning.　　(10)

The sun was bright and yellow. The birds　　(18)

were singing loudly outside her window. Meg　　(25)

looked outside and saw a blue bird sitting　　(33)

in a nest. The nest was high in the tree.　　(43)

Flesch Reading Ease: 99.8
Flesch-Kincaid Grade Level: 0.9

46

Chapter 1 • *Tactics for Boosting Academic Achievement*　　　　Building Vocabulary Using Semantic Mapping

Building Vocabulary Using Semantic Mapping:
Data Recording Sheet (Worksheet)

Student: _____   Grade: _____

Teacher: _____   Date: _____

Semantic components	Possible points	Points earned
Main idea	5	
Category 1	2	
Category 2	2	
Category 3	2	
Category 4	2	
Subcategory 1	1	
Subcategory 2	1	
Subcategory 3	1	
Subcategory 4	1	
Subcategory 5	1	
Subcategory 6	1	
Subcategory 7	1	
Subcategory 8	1	
Total	**21**	

Notes:

Story Sequencing

Objective: This tactic was designed to build sequencing and comprehension skills.

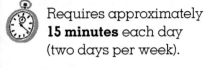

Requires approximately **15 minutes** each day (two days per week).

Materials: Daily folder, any story being read by class (instructional level), Worksheet, timer, pencil, and two Data Recording Sheets as described on the Coach Card.

Preparation: Make copies of tactic reproducibles and gather tactic materials. Make copies of grade-appropriate story.

Teacher design: Teachers may use any story when implementing this tactic. Lengths of stories used are dependent on the reading skill grade level of each student (teacher should have knowledge of levels).

Coach Card

- ❑ Get materials. Go to an assigned practice place. Find the day's story and the Worksheet.

- ❑ **Model**: First, read the story aloud to the student. Next, retell the story by using the following sequencing words: *first, then, next, finally.*

- ❑ **Guided practice**: First, the student reads the story aloud. Next, the student retells the story using the sequencing words. Finally, the student completes the Worksheet by writing down the retelling of the story using the sequence words.

- ❑ **Coach**: Assist the student in grading the Worksheet. Instruct the student to correct mistakes. Document Worksheet results on Worksheet Data Recording Sheet.

- ❑ **Assessment**: Set the timer for one minute. The student should read the passage aloud to the teacher. Instruct the student to stop when the timer buzzes. Instruct the student to tell the teacher what the passage was about, again setting the timer for one minute. Using the Data Recording Sheet (Assessment Component) found at the back of this chapter, the teacher should mark the number of words from the passage that the student uses during the retell.

- ❑ **Coach**: On the Assessment Data Recording Sheet, document the number of words from the passage that the student uses during the retell.

Story Sequencing: Worksheet

Student: _____   Grade: _____

Teacher: _____   Date: _____

First,   _____

_____

_____

_____

_____

Then,   _____

_____

_____

_____

_____

Next,   _____

_____

_____

_____

_____

Finally,   _____

_____

_____

_____

_____

49

Story Sequencing: Data Recording Sheet (Worksheet)

Student: _____   Grade: _____

Teacher: _____   Date: _____

Scoring instructions: A score of 1 should be inserted in each sequence component column when the student demonstrates each component during the retelling of the story. Insert a 0 in the component columns the student does not demonstrate. Calculate and record the total score.

Date	First	Then	Next	Finally	Total completed

Notes:

Making Inferences/Comprehension 1 (Identifying People and Actions)

Objective: This tactic is designed to improve language development (inferring and comprehending).

Materials: Daily folder, Coach Card, 10 or more pictures of people (e.g., classmates, family members, or people from a magazine), timer, and Data Recording Sheet.

Preparation: Make copies of tactic reproducibles and gather remaining tactic materials.

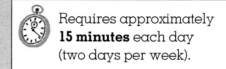

Requires approximately **15 minutes** each day (two days per week).

Coach Card

❑ Get materials. Go to an assigned work area.

Guided practice (use Guided Practice Session section of the Data Recording Sheet):

❑ **Coach**: Present a picture to the student.

❑ **Student**: Verbally identify the person in picture.

❑ **Coach**: Ask the student what the person in the picture is wearing.

❑ **Student**: Describe the clothing that the person in the picture is wearing.

❑ **Coach**: Ask student what the person in the picture is doing.

❑ **Student**: Describe the action being performed in the picture.

❑ **Coach**: Repeat the above process until all pictures are presented and described.

❑ **Assessment**: Set the timer for two minutes. Show the student a picture of a person. Instruct the student to verbally identify the person in picture (male or female, etc.). Ask the student to describe the person (what he/she is wearing, etc.). Ask the student what the person in the picture is doing. When timer buzzes, stop.

❑ **Coach**: Record results in the Assessment Session section of the Data Recording Sheet.

Making Inferences/Comprehension 1
(Identifying People and Actions):
Data Recording Sheet

Student: _____   Grade: _____

Teacher: _____   Date: _____

Guided Practice Session					Assessment Session				
10	10	10	10	10	10	10	10	10	10
9	9	9	9	9	9	9	9	9	9
8	8	8	8	8	8	8	8	8	8
7	7	7	7	7	7	7	7	7	7
6	6	6	6	6	6	6	6	6	6
5	5	5	5	5	5	5	5	5	5
4	4	4	4	4	4	4	4	4	4
3	3	3	3	3	3	3	3	3	3
2	2	2	2	2	2	2	2	2	2
1	1	1	1	1	1	1	1	1	1

Scoring instructions: Each session consists of the presentation of ten pictures. Each picture has a corresponding number on the Data Recording Sheet (i.e., the first picture presented is represented by number 1, the second picture presented is represented by number 2, etc.). Mark incorrect responses by putting a slash (/) through the number. Then place a dot over the correct responses and connect the dots to draw a graph.

Providing Details/Comprehension 2 (Identifying and Describing Objects)

Objective: This tactic is designed to improve written language development (details and comprehension).

Materials: Daily folder, 10 or more pictures of objects from the classroom (magazines can also be used to collect pictures of classroom objects), timer, and Data Recording Sheet.

Preparation: Make copies of tactic reproducibles and gather remaining tactic materials.

 Requires approximately **15 minutes** each day (one or two days per week).

Coach Card

❑ Get materials. Go to an assigned work area.

Guided practice (use Guided Practice Session section of the Data Recording Sheet):

❑ **Coach**: Present a picture to the student.

❑ **Student**: Verbally identify the object in the picture.

❑ **Coach**: Ask the student to describe the color and size of the object.

❑ **Student**: Describe the object in the picture.

❑ **Coach**: Ask the student where the object is located (on a table, a chair, the floor, etc.).

❑ **Student**: Describe the location of the object as it appears in the picture.

❑ **Coach**: Ask the student to identify the physical location of the object within the classroom.

❑ **Student**: Find the object in the classroom.

❑ **Coach**: Repeat the above process until all pictures are presented, described, and located.

❑ **Assessment**: Set the timer for two minutes. Present the student with a picture of an object. Instruct the student to describe the object (color, size, shape, etc.). Instruct the student to describe the location of the object. Have the student explain what the object is used for. When the timer buzzes, stop.

❑ **Coach**: Record results in the Assessment Session section of the Data Recording Sheet.

Providing Details/Comprehension 2
(Identifying and Describing Objects):
Data Recording Sheet

Student: _____ Grade: _____

Teacher: _____ Date: _____

Guided Practice Session						**Assessment Session**				
10	10	10	10	10		10	10	10	10	10
9	9	9	9	9		9	9	9	9	9
8	8	8	8	8		8	8	8	8	8
7	7	7	7	7		7	7	7	7	7
6	6	6	6	6		6	6	6	6	6
5	5	5	5	5		5	5	5	5	5
4	4	4	4	4		4	4	4	4	4
3	3	3	3	3		3	3	3	3	3
2	2	2	2	2		2	2	2	2	2
1	1	1	1	1		1	1	1	1	1

Scoring instructions: Each session consists of the presentation of ten pictures. Each picture has a corresponding number on the Data Recording Sheet (i.e., the first picture presented is represented by number 1, the second picture presented is represented by number 2, etc.). Mark incorrect responses by putting a slash (/) through the number. Then place a dot over the correct responses and connect the dots to draw a graph.

Improving Comprehension Using Group Discussion

Objective: This tactic is designed to improve reading comprehension.

Materials: Daily folder, reading passage (any text; see Sample of Narrative Text), worksheet of questions (see Sample Questions for Narrative Text) or questions provided in textbook, timer, pencil, and two Data Recording Sheets as described on the Coach Card.

 Requires approximately **45–60 minutes** for tactic implementation (one or two times per week).

Preparation: Teacher should form groups (six students in each) made up of an equal number of students with higher- and lower-functioning reading levels. Make copies of tactic reproducibles and gather remaining tactic materials. Prepare a daily folder for each group of students. Make copies of a selected reading passage and a prepared set of questions pertaining to the reading passage (include literal, inferential, and critical).

Note: Prior to using this tactic's Coach Card, read passage to/with students.

Coach Card

- ❏ Get materials.
- ❏ **Coach**: Encourage a group discussion of the reading passage. (Teacher should withdraw from the discussion as soon as possible. Allow the discussion to end before going to the next step).
- ❏ **Coach**: Break six-person groups into two triads.
- ❏ **Coach**: Present one copy of the set of questions to each group member.
- ❏ **Triads**: Discuss the story within the small groups and divide questions equally among the members.
- ❏ **Triads**: Present the questions and allow time for group members to discuss.
- ❏ **Triads**: Add new questions to the list to address points that are thought to be important.
- ❏ **Triads**: Write answers to the questions and discussion points on paper.
- ❏ **Coach**: Bring students together for presentation of their answers.
- ❏ **Triads**: Present and discuss answers with the rest of the class.
- ❏ **Coach**: Encourage all students to offer alternative responses representing different points of view.
- ❏ **Coach**: Model exemplary reasoning and discussion practices.
- ❏ **Coach**: Complete a Worksheet Data Recording Sheet for each group and place it in each group's daily folder.
- ❏ **Assessment**: Set the timer for one minute. The student should read the passage aloud to the teacher. Instruct the student to stop when the timer buzzes. Instruct the student to tell the teacher what the passage was about, again setting the timer for one minute. Using the Data Recording Sheet (Assessment Component) found at the back of this chapter, the teacher should mark the number of words from the passage that the student uses during the retell.
- ❏ **Coach**: On the Assessment Data Recording Sheet, document the number of words from the passage that the student uses during the retell.

Improving Comprehension Using Group Discussion: Sample of Narrative Text

> Meg is moving again; this is something she does every three years. It is not her idea to move; she must move because of her father's job. Her father is an officer in the United States Navy. A naval officer manages groups of sailors to make sure they do their jobs properly. The navy moves sailors often in order to provide them with a vast amount of experience in different jobs around the world. Meg is 11 years old, and she has lived in California, Florida, Virginia, Louisiana, and Texas. Meg always gets nervous when moving, and she is often sad when leaving her friends. However, she loves living in different parts of the United States and experiencing the different cultures. Meg always adjusts to her new surroundings and always makes friends. She has many friends throughout the United States. She tries to keep in touch with her friends. Meg is proud of her dad and knows his job helps keep us free.
>
> *Flesch-Kincaid Grade Level: 6.0*

Sample Questions for Narrative Text

1. What does Meg's father do for a living?
   Meg's father is a United States naval officer.

2. What are some emotions Meg feels when moving?
   Meg feels nervous, sad, and excited.

3. Why does Meg's father's job transfer him every three years?
   The military transfers sailors as a way of providing them with a vast amount of experience in different jobs around the world.

4. What does a naval officer do?
   A naval officer manages a group of sailors.

5. What does it mean to be "free?"
   Having the ability to do, act, or think as one pleases.

Improving Comprehension Using Group Discussion: Data Recording Sheet (Worksheet)

Group members: _____   Grade: _____

Teacher: _____   Date: _____

Components	Subcomponents	Possible points	Points earned
Group discussion	Did group members participate?	5	
Division of questions	Did group members work together?	5	
Triad discussion	Did all members participate?	5	
Formation of additional questions	Did questions pertain to reading material?	5	
Answers	Were answers relevant and was support provided?	10	
Presentation	Did all members give input?	5	
	Total		

Notes:

Improving Comprehension Using MULTIPASS

Objective: This tactic is designed to improve reading comprehension of expository text.

Materials: Daily folder, expository text passage (i.e., choose chapter in science or social studies textbook; see Sample Expository Text Passage), Worksheet, timer, pencil, and Data Recording Sheet (Assessment Component) found at the back of this chapter.

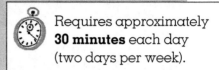 Requires approximately **30 minutes** each day (two days per week).

Preparation: Make copies of tactic reproducibles and gather remaining tactic materials. Make copies of expository text passage (chapter of textbook).

Coach Card

❑ Get materials and go to an assigned work area. Take out the Worksheet and Sample Expository Text or other text passage.

❑ **First PASS**: Instruct the student to skim through selected pages to become familiar with the main idea and organization.

❑ **Second PASS**: Instruct the student to read through and answer questions (by guessing) at the end of the chapter.

❑ **Third PASS**: Instruct the student to read through the text.

❑ **Self-test**: Instruct the student, now with newly acquired information, to answer questions at the end of chapter.

❑ **Assessment**: Set the timer for one minute. The student should read the passage aloud to the teacher. Instruct the student to stop when the timer buzzes. Instruct the student to tell the teacher what the passage was about, again setting the timer for one minute. Using the Data Recording Sheet (Assessment Component) found at the back of this chapter, the teacher should mark the number of words from the passage that the student uses during the retell.

58

Chapter 1 • *Tactics for Boosting Academic Achievement*

Improving Comprehension Using MULTIPASS

Improving Comprehension Using MULTIPASS: Sample Expository Text Passage

The Ways the Earth's Surface Has Changed

Continental drift

Findings from years of scientific research tell us that the Earth has not always looked the way it does now. The continents found on Earth have not always been positioned as they are today. The surface of the Earth is constantly moving because of what is called continental drift. *Continental drift* is the term used to describe the theory of how Earth's continents move over its surface.

About 225 million years ago, all the land on Earth was connected in one "supercontinent" called Pangea. Scientific evidence suggests that about 200 million years ago, Pangea split into two big continents. To this day, the continents are still moving. Millions of years from now, Earth will look a lot different.

History told through rocks

The Grand Canyon, which is two billion years old, is made up of layers of sedimentary rock. Sedimentary rock is formed from sediments that have cemented together over time. The Grand Canyon is a mile deep. The Colorado River has cut deeply through the 20 different layers of sedimentary rock, forming numerous steep-walled canyons. Forests are found at higher elevations, while the lower elevations are comprised of a series of desert basins.

Well known for its geologic significance, the Grand Canyon is one of the most studied geologic landscapes in the world. It offers an excellent record of three of the four eras of geological time, a rich and diverse fossil record, a vast array of geologic features and rock types, and numerous caves containing extensive and significant geological, paleontological, archeological, and biological resources.

Contained within the canyon's walls of sedimentary rock is a fossil record of organisms from the Earth's earliest time. A fossil is the remains of past life found in sedimentary rock. Fossils are studied by scientists to find out how life on Earth has changed over the years.

What do fossils teach us?

Fossils are the remains or traces of plants and animals that lived a long time ago—or the evidence of those plants and animals. Scientists have found fossils to show us that life on Earth is a lot different today than it was years ago. Fossils found provide us with facts regarding the various types of animals that once roamed the Earth.

Fossils also show that the Earth's surface is a lot different today than it once was. Fossils of sea organisms have been found on top of high mountains, which implies that those areas were once under water.

Improving Comprehension Using MULTIPASS   *Tactics for Boosting Academic Achievement* • Chapter 1

Improving Comprehension Using MULTIPASS: Sample Worksheet

Student: __Meghan__   Grade: __6__

Teacher: __Mrs. Stephens__   Date: __March 15__

Title:	The Ways the Earth's Surface Has Changed

First PASS

Notes:

1. Earth's surface
2. Rocks
3. Fossils
4. _____

Second PASS

Notes:

1. Pangea is a continent.
2. The oldest rocks in the Grand Canyon are thousands of years old.
3. We learn from the past through fossils.
4. _____

Third PASS

Notes:

1. Pangea—Earth joined together as a "supercontinent" 225 million years ago.
2. Rocks on the Grand Canyon are nearly two billion years old.
3. Fossils are remains of past life.
4. _____

Improving Comprehension Using MULTIPASS: Worksheet

Student: _____   Grade: _____

Teacher: _____   Date: _____

Title:

First PASS

Notes:

1._____

2._____

3._____

4._____

Second PASS

Notes:

1._____

2._____

3._____

4._____

Third PASS

Notes:

1._____

2._____

3._____

4._____

Improving Comprehension Using ASK IT

Objective: This tactic is designed to increase reading comprehension by teaching students self-question techniques to use during reading.

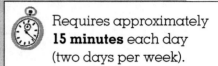 Requires approximately **15 minutes** each day (two days per week).

Materials: Daily folder, paper, pencil, grade-appropriate reading material (i.e., choose from any textbook being used in classroom), timer, Worksheet, and two Data Recording Sheets as described on the Coach Card.

Preparation: Make copies of tactic reproducibles and gather remaining tactic materials. Make copies of grade-appropriate reading material (any textbook being used in class or reading passage accessible to teacher).

Coach Card

❑ Get materials. Go to an assigned work area. Write names, grade, and date on Worksheet.

❑ **Model: A—ATTEND** to clues when reading. (1) What is the title of the passage? (2) What do the pictures tell you? (3) What do the words in the first sentence tell you? (Write in your own words.)

❑ **Model: S—SAY**: Develop a question about a clue (write it on a piece of paper).

❑ **Model: K—KEEP** a prediction in mind, based on the question you developed.

❑ **Model: I—IDENTIFY**: (1) Find the answers while reading. (2) Write the answer on the paper.

❑ **Model: T—TALK**: Discuss how you got your answer with the teacher.

❑ Place completed paragraph, answers, and Worksheet in your daily folder for the teacher to evaluate.

❑ **Coach**: Assist the student in evaluating the paragraph using the Worksheet Data Recording Sheet.

❑ **Coach**: Review and score worksheet. Write student scores on the Worksheet Data Recording Sheet at the end of this tactic.

❑ **Assessment**: Set the timer for one minute. The student should read the passage aloud to the teacher. Instruct the student to stop when the timer buzzes. Instruct the student to tell the teacher what the passage was about, again setting the timer for one minute. Using the Data Recording Sheet (Assessment Component) found at the back of this chapter, the teacher should mark the number of words from the passage that the student uses during the retell.

❑ **Coach**: On the Assessment Data Recording Sheet, document the number of words from the passage that the student uses during the retell.

Improving Comprehension Using ASK IT: Worksheet

Student: _____ Grade: _____

Teacher: _____ Date: _____

A—ATTEND to clues when reading.

   (1) What is the name of the passage?

   _____

   _____

   (2) What do the pictures tell you?

   _____

   _____

   (3) What do the words in the first sentence of the passage tell you?

   _____

   _____

S —SAY

   Write a question using a clue.

   _____

   _____

K—KEEP

   What is your prediction?

   _____

   _____

I —IDENTIFY

   Find details supporting your prediction.

   _____

   _____

T —TALK

   Discuss with the teacher how you got your answer.

63

Improving Comprehension Using ASK IT:
Data Recording Sheet (Worksheet)*

Student: _____ Grade: _____

Teacher: _____ Date: _____

ASK IT components	ASK IT subcomponents	Possible points	Points earned
A—ATTEND	What is the title of the passage?	5	
	What do the pictures tell you?	5	
	What do the words in the first sentence tell you?	5	
S—SAY	Develop a question about the clue.	5	
K—KEEP	Make a prediction.	5	
I—IDENTIFY	Find and write answers.	5	
T—TELL	Explain to teacher how you got the answer.	5	
	Total	**35**	

Notes:

Improving Comprehension Using Hit and Miss

Objective: This tactic is designed to teach students to monitor what they read and to recognize the information in the text they know about and the information they have difficulty with.

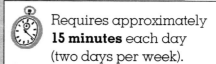
Requires approximately **15 minutes** each day (two days per week).

Materials: Daily folder, grade-appropriate reading passage (choose from science or social studies textbooks), timer, Worksheet, Fix-It Strategy Cards, pencil, two Data Recording Sheets as described on the Coach Card, and dictionary.

Preparation: Make copies of tactic reproducibles and gather remaining tactic materials. Make copies of the reading passage. Attach the copy of the Fix-It Strategy Cards on the inside front cover of the folder. Teach students that a **hit** is something you get or understand, and a **miss** is something you do not understand. Explain that a miss might involve an unfamiliar vocabulary word or a lack of understanding of what the author is saying.

Coach Card

- ❏ Get materials. Go to an assigned work area. Find the Worksheet and the reading passage.

- ❏ Write names, grade, and date on the Worksheet.

- ❏ Read the passage. Circle any words you do not know

- ❏ On the Worksheet, write any misses you circled in the passage.

- ❏ Use the following Fix-It Strategies to repair each miss. (These steps should be performed with a coach's assistance. If necessary, the coach should provide feedback by giving examples and non-examples for each step.)

  - ○ (1) Reread the sentence containing the miss and the sentences before and after the miss.

  - ○ (2) Reread the sentence without the word.

  - ○ (3) Tell the coach what word makes sense in the sentence.

  - ○ (4) Look for a prefix or suffix in the word that might help determine the meaning of the word. Write this on your Worksheet.

- ○ (5) Break the word apart and look for smaller words. Write these smaller words on your Worksheet.

- ○ (6) On the Worksheet, write the meaning of each miss. Use the dictionary if you need help.

- ❏ **Coach**: Assist the student in reviewing and scoring the Worksheet. Allow student to correct any mistakes. Write student scores on the Worksheet Data Recording Sheet at the end of this tactic.

- ❏ **Assessment**: Set the timer for one minute. The student should read the passage aloud to the teacher. Instruct the student to stop when the timer buzzes. Instruct the student to tell the teacher what the passage was about, again setting the timer for one minute. Using the Data Recording Sheet (Assessment Component) found at the back of this chapter, the teacher should mark the number of words from the passage that the student uses during the retell.

- ❏ **Coach**: On the Assessment Data Recording Sheet, document the number of words from the passage that the student uses during the retell.

Improving Comprehension Using Hit and Miss:
Data Recording Sheet (Worksheet)

Student: _____   Grade: _____

Teacher: _____   Date: _____

Word missed	Prefix	Suffix	Smaller words	Meaning of word

Notes:

Improving Comprehension Using Get the Gist

Objective: This tactic is designed to help students determine the main idea of a passage and rephrase important points of a text using 20 words or less.

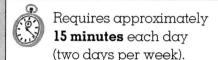 Requires approximately **15 minutes** each day (two days per week).

Materials: Daily folder, grade-appropriate reading passages of not more than three paragraphs (one per Coach Card; choose from science or social studies textbooks), timer, Worksheet, pencil, and two Data Recording Sheets as described on the Coach Card.

Preparation: Make copies of tactic reproducibles and gather remaining tactic materials. Make copies of the selected reading passages and attach a copy of the Worksheet to each.

Note: This tactic can be implemented with individuals, small groups, or large groups.

Coach Card

- ❑ Get materials. Go to an assigned work area. Find the Worksheet and reading passage.
- ❑ Write names, grade, and date on the Worksheet.
- ❑ Read the passage silently.
- ❑ While reading, think about what the story is mostly about.
- ❑ Complete the Worksheet using the following criteria:
  - ○ (1) Place a check mark on the passage next to the word that best describes what the passage is about.
  - ○ (2) Write the name of the person, place, or thing the passage is about.
  - ○ (3) Write the most important point made in the passage about the person, place, or thing.
  - ○ (4) Using fewer than 20 words, rephrase the important point made in the passage.
- ❑ Score your Worksheet using the Worksheet Data Recording Sheet.
- ❑ **Assessment**: Set the timer for one minute. The student should read the passage aloud to the teacher. Instruct the student to stop when the timer buzzes. Instruct the student to tell the teacher what the passage was about, again setting the timer for one minute. Using the Data Recording Sheet (Assessment Component) found at the back of this chapter, the teacher should mark the number of words from the passage that the student uses during the retell.
- ❑ **Coach**: On the Assessment Data Recording Sheet, document the number of words from the passage that the student uses during the retell.

Improving Comprehension Using Get the Gist: Worksheet

Student: _____ Grade: _____

Teacher: _____ Date: _____

Instructions: Read the passage silently. Write 20 words that describe the information you read in the passage.

_____	_____	_____	_____
_____	_____	_____	_____
_____	_____	_____	_____
_____	_____	_____	_____
_____	_____	_____	_____

In 20 words or less, write a summary of the passage.

_____

_____

_____

_____

_____

_____

_____

Improving Comprehension Using Get the Gist: Data Recording Sheet (Worksheet)

Student: _____ Grade: _____

Teacher: _____ Date begun:_____

Date ended:_____

Scoring instructions: Award one point in each blank under the corresponding skill.

Date	Student checked the word that best described what the passage was about	Student was able to write the name of the person, place, or thing the passage was about	Student was able to write about the most important point made in the passage	Student was able to use 20 words or less to rephrase the important point made in the passage	Total points

Notes:

Improving Comprehension Using TRAVEL

Objective: This tactic is designed to increase reading comprehension by teaching students how to organize material they read.

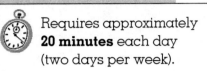
Requires approximately **20 minutes** each day (two days per week).

Materials:: Daily folder, grade-appropriate reading material, Worksheet, timer, pencil, and two Data Recording Sheets as described on the Coach Card.

Preparation: Make copies of tactic reproducibles and gather remaining tactic materials. Make copies of grade-appropriate reading material (i.e., from textbook) and attach a Worksheet to each reading passage. Write the topic at the top of the Worksheet.

Coach Card

- ❏ Get materials. Go to an assigned work area. Find the Worksheet with attached reading passage.

- ❏ Write names, grade, and date on the worksheet.

- ❏ **Model**: Write the **T** (TOPIC) on the Worksheet and circle it.

- ❏ **Model**: **R** (READ) a paragraph.

- ❏ **Model**: **A** (ASK) what the main idea and three details are and write them down.

- ❏ **Model**: **V** (VERIFY) the main idea by circling it and linking it to the details.

- ❏ **Model**: **E** (EXAMINE) the next paragraph and Ask and Verify again.

- ❏ **Model**: **L** (LINK) all the circles when you're finished with the story. Write a short summary of the main idea of the entire passage.

- ❏ **Student**: When finished, score your paper with the help of the teacher. Correct your mistakes. Document results on the Worksheet Data Recording Sheet.

- ❏ **Assessment**: Set the timer for one minute. The student should read the passage aloud to the teacher. Instruct the student to stop when the timer buzzes. Instruct the student to tell the teacher what the passage was about, again setting the timer for one minute. Using the Data Recording Sheet (Assessment Component) found at the back of this chapter, the teacher should mark the number of words from the passage that the student uses during the retell.

- ❏ **Coach**: On the Assessment Data Recording Sheet, document the number of words from the passage that the student uses during the retell.

Improving Comprehension Using TRAVEL:
Sample Reading Passage

Plants make their own food by using water, carbon dioxide, chlorophyll, and sunlight. The process by which plants make food is called photosynthesis. *Photo* means "light" and *synthesis* means "putting." In photosynthesis, plants put together materials to make food with the energy of the sunlight.

Photosynthesis takes place mainly in a plant's leaves. Certain cells in the leaf have most of the leaf's chloroplasts. These structures contain chlorophyll, the pigment that gives plants their green color.

Flesch-Kincaid Grade Level: 7.1

Improving Comprehension Using TRAVEL:
Sample Worksheet

Student: <u>Hannah</u>   Grade: <u>5th</u>

Teacher: <u>Ms. Tammy</u>   Date: <u>July 21</u>

Topic: <u>Photosynthesis</u>

Main idea: <u>Plants use the process of photosynthesis to create food and survive.</u>

Details:

1. <u>Plants use water, carbon dioxide, chlorophyll, and sunlight to make food.</u>

2. <u>Photosynthesis occurs mainly in the plant's leaves.</u>

3. <u>Chlorophyll gives plants their green color.</u>

Link:

<u>All plants go through a process called "photosynthesis" to create food</u>
<u>and survive. Plants use water, carbon dioxide, chlorophyll, and sunlight to</u>
<u>make food. Photosynthesis occurs mainly in the plant's leaves. Chlorophyll</u>
<u>gives plants their green color. Plants could not survive without the process</u>
<u>of photosynthesis.</u>

Improving Comprehension Using TRAVEL: Sample Data Recording Sheet

Student: Hannah   Grade: 5th

Teacher: Ms. Tammy   Date begun: July 21

Date ended: _____

Scoring instructions: Insert the date in the appropriate column. For each TRAVEL component completed correctly, place a 1 in the corresponding column. For each TRAVEL component answered incorrectly, place a 0 in the corresponding column. Tally up and record the total number of points.

Date	T TOPIC	R READ	A ASK	V VERIFY	E EXAMINE	L LINK	TOTAL
7/21/05	1	1	1	1	1	1	6 / 6

Notes:

Improving Comprehension Using TRAVEL:
Worksheet

Student: _____   Grade: _____

Teacher: _____   Date: _____

Topic: _____

Main idea: _____

_____

_____

Details:

   1. _____

      _____

   2. _____

      _____

   3. _____

      _____

Link:

_____

_____

_____

_____

_____

_____

_____

_____

Improving Comprehension Using TRAVEL: Data Recording Sheet (Worksheet)

Student: _____   Grade: _____

Teacher: _____   Date begun: _____

Date ended: _____

Scoring instructions: Insert the date in the appropriate column. For each TRAVEL component completed correctly, place a 1 in the corresponding column. For each TRAVEL component answered incorrectly, place a 0 in the corresponding column. Tally up and record the total number of points.

Date	T TOPIC	R READ	A ASK	V VERIFY	E EXAMINE	L LINK	TOTAL

Notes:

Improving Comprehension Using K-W-L

Objective: This tactic is designed to increase reading comprehension.

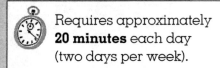
Requires approximately **20 minutes** each day (two days per week).

Materials: Daily folder, grade-appropriate expository reading material, Worksheet, timer, pencil, and two Data Recording Sheets as described on the Coach Card.

Preparation: Make copies of tactic reproducibles and gather remaining tactic materials. Make copies of grade-appropriate reading materials (one chapter of a textbook or a short reading passage) and attach a Worksheet to each reading page. Write the title of the passage at the top of the Worksheet.

Coach Card

- ❑ Get materials. Go to an assigned work area. Find the day's Worksheet and attached reading page. Write names, grade, and date on the Worksheet.
- ❑ **Model**: Read the topic written on the Worksheet.
- ❑ **Model**: Complete the **K** (KNOW) section of the Worksheet with items you know about the topic.
- ❑ **Model**: Complete the **W** (WHAT) section of the Worksheet with items you want to know about the topic.
- ❑ **Model**: Read the reading passage.
- ❑ **Model**: Complete the **L** (LEARNED) section of the Worksheet with items you learned after reading the passage.
- ❑ **Coach**: Present the student with the reading passage and KWL Strategy Worksheet. Instruct the student to read the passage and complete the Worksheet.
- ❑ **Student**: Score your paper with the help of the teacher and write the number correct at the top of the page. Correct your mistakes.
- ❑ **Coach**: Write the score on the Worksheet Data Recording Sheet.
- ❑ **Assessment**: Set the timer for one minute. The student should read the passage aloud to the teacher. Instruct the student to stop when the timer buzzes. Instruct the student to tell the teacher what the passage was about, again setting the timer for one minute. Using the Data Recording Sheet (Assessment Component) found at the back of this chapter, the teacher should mark the number of words from the passage that the student uses during the retell.
- ❑ **Coach**: On the Assessment Data Recording Sheet, document the number of words from the passage that the student uses during the retell.

76

Chapter 1 • *Tactics for Boosting Academic Achievement*   Improving Comprehension Using K-W-L

Improving Comprehension Using K-W-L: Worksheet

Student: _____ Grade: _____

Teacher: _____ Date: _____

Topic: _____

K   What do you already KNOW about this topic?

_____

_____

_____

W   WHAT do you want to learn? WHAT do you think the reading will
be about? (Scan text for two minutes.)

_____

_____

_____

(Read entire passage or page.)

L   What are the most important things you LEARNED? List the
predictions that were correct.

_____

_____

_____

Improving Comprehension Using K-W-L:
Data Recording Sheet (Worksheet)

Student: _____   Grade: _____

Teacher: _____   Date begun: _____

Date ended: _____

Scoring instructions: Place a plus sign (+) in each column answered.

Date	K KNOW	W WHAT	L LEARNED

Notes:

Improving Comprehension Using the PEP Strategy

Objective: This tactic is designed to help students comprehend reading materials by organizing data and asking questions during reading.

Materials: Daily folder, grade-appropriate reading material, paper, pencil, timer, PEP Strategy Worksheet, and two Data Recording Sheets as described on the Coach Card.

 Requires approximately **15 minutes** each day (two days per week).

Preparation: Make copies of tactic reproducibles and gather remaining tactic materials. Make copies of selected grade-appropriate reading material (or use a textbook the student is using in the classroom).

Coach Card

- ❑ Get materials. Go to an assigned work area.
- ❑ **Model**: Read the passage.
- ❑ **Model**: **P**—PERSON (man or woman, boy or girl?)
  - ○ What did he/she do?
  - ○ Why did he/she do it?
  - ○ When and where was it done?
  - ○ What are the important words?
- ❑ **Model**: **E**—EVENT (something happened?)
  - ○ What happened?
  - ○ Why did it happen?
  - ○ When and where did it happen?
  - ○ Who was involved?
  - ○ What are the important words?
- ❑ **Model**: **P**—PLACE (location?)
  - ○ Where is it?
  - ○ What is it like?
  - ○ Why is it special?
  - ○ What are the important words?
- ❑ **Coach**: Present the student with the reading passage and PEP Strategy Worksheet. Instruct the student to read the passage and complete the Worksheet.

- ❑ **Student**: Score your paper with the teacher's help and write the number correct at the top of the page. Correct your mistakes.
- ❑ **Coach**: Evaluate the student's answers using the Worksheet Data Recording Sheet.
- ❑ **Assessment**: Set the timer for one minute. The student should read the passage aloud to the teacher. Instruct the student to stop when the timer buzzes. Instruct the student to tell the teacher what the passage was about, again setting the timer for one minute. Using the Data Recording Sheet (Assessment Component) found at the back of this chapter, the teacher should mark the number of words from the passage that the student uses during the retell.
- ❑ **Coach**: On the Assessment Data Recording Sheet, document the number of words from the passage that the student uses during the retell.

Improving Comprehension Using the PEP Strategy: Worksheet

Student: _____   Grade: _____

Teacher: _____   Date: _____

P—PERSON (man or woman, boy or girl?)

    What did he/she do? _____

    Why did he/she do it? _____

    When and where was it done? _____

    What are the important words? _____

E—EVENT (something happened?)

    What happened? _____

    Why did it happen? _____

    When and where did it happen? _____

    Where did it happen? _____

    Who was involved? _____

    What are the important words? _____

P—PLACE (location?)

    Where is it?_____

    What is it like? _____

    Why is it special? _____

    What are the important words? _____

Improving Comprehension Using the PEP Strategy: Data Recording Sheet (Worksheet)

Student: _____ Grade: _____

Teacher: _____ Date: _____

PEP components	Subcomponents	Possible points	Points earned
P—PERSON	What did he/she do?	5	
	Why did he/she do it?	5	
	When/where was it done?	5	
	Important words	5	
E—EVENT	What happened?	5	
	When/where did it happen?	5	
	Who was involved?	5	
	Important words	5	
P—PLACE	Where is it?	5	
	What is it like?	5	
	Why is it special?	5	
	Total	**60**	

Notes:

Improving Comprehension Using PREVIEW

Objective: This tactic is designed to generate interest in and enthusiasm for what students are about to read by stimulating background knowledge and providing an opportunity to hypothesize.

 Requires approximately **20 minutes** each day (one to two days per week).

Materials: Daily folder, timer, grade-appropriate reading passages, Worksheet, pencil, and two Data Recording Sheets as described on the Coach Card.

Preparation: Make copies of tactic reproducibles and gather remaining tactic materials. Make copies of selected grade-appropriate reading passages (classroom textbooks may be used) and attach a Worksheet to each reading passage.

Coach Card

- ❏ Get materials. Go to an assigned work area. Find the day's reading passage and attached Worksheet.
- ❏ Write names, grade, and date on the Worksheet.
- ❏ Check off each of the next seven steps as they are completed.
- ❏ **Model**: Read the title of the passage silently.
- ❏ **Model**: Check the passage to see if there are any pictures, diagrams, or tables to help better understand the passage.
- ❏ **Model**: Read each heading and think about what it means.
- ❏ **Model**: Look for key words in bold print, underlined, or italicized, and think about what they tell you about the passage.
- ❏ **Model**: Read the first and last sentence of the passage.
- ❏ **Model**: Complete Part 1 of the Worksheet. Write the title of the passage and your prediction of what the passage is about.
- ❏ **Model**: Read the entire passage.

- ❏ **Model**: Complete Part 2 of the Worksheet.
- ❏ **Coach**: Present the student with a reading passage and Worksheet. Instruct the student to read the passage, complete the Worksheet, and return the Worksheet to you for scoring.
- ❏ **Coach**: Record the results on the Worksheet Data Recording Sheet. Place completed work in the student's daily folder.
- ❏ **Assessment**: Set the timer for one minute. The student should read the passage aloud to the teacher. Instruct the student to stop when the timer buzzes. Instruct the student to tell the teacher what the passage was about, again setting the timer for one minute. Using the Data Recording Sheet (Assessment Component) found at the back of this chapter, the teacher should mark the number of words from the passage that the student uses during the retell.
- ❏ **Coach**: On the Assessment Data Recording Sheet, document the number of words from the passage that the student uses during the retell.

Improving Comprehension Using PREVIEW: Worksheet

Student: _____ Grade: _____

Teacher: _____ Date: _____

Title of passage: _____

PART 1   My prediction: _____

_____

_____

_____

_____

_____   **STOP**

PART 2

READ PASSAGE

Was your prediction correct? Explain. _____

_____

_____

_____   **STOP**

What helped you make your prediction? _____

_____

_____

_____

Improving Comprehension Using PREVIEW:
Data Recording Sheet (Worksheet)

Student: _____ Grade: _____

Teacher: _____ Date begun: _____

Date ended: _____

Scoring instructions: Place a check mark in the appropriate box.

Date	Prediction made correctly	Prediction made incorrectly

Notes:

Improving Comprehension Using Ask Questions

Objective: This tactic is designed to generate interest and enthusiasm and improve reading comprehension by encouraging students to ask questions before, during, and after reading occurs.

 Requires approximately **20 minutes** each day (one to two days per week).

Materials: Daily folder, grade-appropriate reading passages, timer, multi-page Worksheet, and pencil.

Preparation: Make copies of tactic reproducibles and gather remaining tactic materials. Make copies of selected grade-appropriate reading passages (classroom textbooks may be used) and attach a Coach Card and a Worksheet to each reading passage. Prepare a daily folder containing all sets of reading passages and sheets.

Coach Card

- ❑ Get materials. Go to an assigned work area Find the day's reading passage and attached Worksheet pages. Write names, grade, and date on the first page of the Worksheet.

- ❑ Read just the title of the passage silently, then stop.

- ❑ Answer questions 1–4 on the Worksheet.

- ❑ Begin reading the text of the passage.

- ❑ While reading, answer questions 5–7 on the Worksheet.

- ❑ Finish reading the passage.

- ❑ Answer questions 8–12 on the Worksheet after reading is completed. Review your answers.

- ❑ **Coach**: Score the Worksheet through discussion with teacher and correct any mistakes.

- ❑ **Assessment**: Set the timer for one minute. The student should read the passage aloud to the teacher. Instruct the student to stop when the timer buzzes. Again, set the timer for one minute; instruct the student should tell the teacher what the passage was about, and the teacher should mark the number of words from the passage that the student uses during the retell.

- ❑ **Coach**: On the Assessment Data Recording Sheet at the end of this chapter, document the number of words from the passage that the student uses during the retell.

Improving Comprehension Using Ask Questions: Worksheet

Student: _____ Grade: _____

Teacher: _____ Date: _____

Before reading:

1. What is the purpose for reading this passage? _____

   _____

   _____

   _____

2. What do I already know about this topic? _____

   _____

   _____

   _____

3. What do I think I will learn about this topic? _____

   _____

   _____

   _____

4. What are my predictions? _____

   _____

   _____

   _____

During reading:

5. Does what I am reading make sense? _____

   _____

6. Is this what I expected? Should I revise my predictions or suspend judgment

   until later?_____

   _____

   _____

7. How are the important points related to one another? What parts are similar or different? _____

_____

_____

After reading:

8. What were the most important points? _____

_____

_____

_____

9. Which sections supported these points? _____

_____

_____

_____

_____

10. What is my opinion? How do I feel? Do I agree or disagree? _____

_____

_____

_____

_____

11. What new information did I learn? _____

_____

_____

_____

_____

12. Should I reread for better understanding? Are there other strategies that I should use? _____

_____

_____

_____

Improving Comprehension Using Story Structure

Objective: This tactic is designed to improve students' reading comprehension through the use of story Structure.

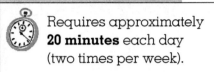

Requires approximately **20 minutes** each day (two times per week).

Materials: Daily folder, Worksheet, chapter in classroom textbook or short story, pencil, timer, and two Data Recording Sheets as described on the Coach Card.

Preparation: Make copies of tactic reproducibles and gather remaining tactic materials. Make one copy of the reading material selected by the teacher and attach a Worksheet. For assessment purposes, make copies of three selected stories from the student's independent and/or instructional reading level and attach a Worksheet to each reading passage.

Coach Card

❑ Get materials. Go to an assigned work area. Find the day's story and attached Worksheet.

❑ Write names, grade, and date on the Worksheet.

❑ **Model**: Read the story silently.

❑ **Model**: Read over the questions on the Worksheet.

❑ **Model**: Complete each question by writing your answer in complete sentences.

❑ **Coach**: Beginning with Story 1, provide the student with one level reading passage and Worksheet, and have him/her fill in the names, grade, and date on the top of the Worksheet. Instruct the student to read the story silently, and then read over the Worksheet.

❑ **Coach**: Instruct student to complete the Worksheet.

❑ **Student**: Score the Worksheet with the help of the teacher.

❑ **Coach**: Record correct responses by placing a check mark next to the component answered correctly on the Worksheet Data Recording Sheet. Place completed work in the student's daily folder.

❑ **Assessment**: Set the timer for one minute. The student should read the passage aloud to the teacher. Instruct the student to stop when the timer buzzes. Instruct the student to tell the teacher what the passage was about, again setting the timer for one minute. Using the Data Recording Sheet (Assessment Component) found at the back of this chapter, the teacher should mark the number of words from the passage that the student uses during the retell.

❑ **Coach**: On the Assessment Data Recording Sheet, document the number of words from the passage that the student uses during the retell.

Improving Comprehension Using Story Structure: Worksheet

Student: _____   Grade: _____

Teacher: _____   Date: _____

Name of story: _____

1. Name the problem or conflict. _____

    _____

    _____

2. Identify the main characters and describe them. _____

    _____

    _____

3. Where does the story take place?_____

    _____

    _____

4. Identify other characters and describe them. _____

    _____

    _____

5. Is there an added twist or complication in the story? _____

    _____

    _____

6. Tell how the problem is or is not solved. _____

    _____

    _____

7. What is the theme of the story? What is the author trying to say? _____

    _____

    _____

Improving Comprehension Using Story Structure: Data Recording Sheet (Worksheet)

Student: _____   Grade: _____

Teacher: _____   Date begun: _____

                                                       Date ended: _____

Scoring instructions: For each story read and Worksheet completed, place a check mark in the column next to the correctly answered component.

Story components	Story 1 Date: _____	Story 2 Date: _____	Story 3 Date: _____
1. Main idea (problem/conflict)			
2. Main character(s)			
3. Setting			
4. Other characters			
5. Problem (added twists/complications)			
6. Solution			
7. Theme			

Notes:

Improving Comprehension Using Story Maps

Objective: This tactic is designed to improve students' reading comprehension through the use of mapping concepts.

Materials: Daily folder, Worksheet, grade-level stories (short story or classroom text), pencil, timer, and two Data Recording Sheets as described on the Coach Card.

Preparation: Make copies of tactic reproducibles and gather tactic materials. Make copies of reading passage selected from the student's independent and/or instructional reading level. Attach a Worksheet to the reading passage.

 Requires approximately **20 minutes** each day (one to two days per week).

Coach Card

❑ Get materials. Go to an assigned work area. Find the day's story and attached Worksheet.

❑ Complete the following mapping concepts (teacher should circle those that are appropriate): Main Character, Other Characters, Setting, Problem, and Solution.

❑ Write name, grade, and date on the Worksheet.

❑ Write the title of the passage on the Worksheet.

❑ Read the story silently and then look at the Worksheet.

❑ Write the main character's name in the center circle on the Worksheet.

❑ Using the main character given in the center circle, complete the outer circles by writing words or sentences relating to the concepts the teacher has circled above.

❑ **Coach**: Give feedback and help the student make needed corrections.

❑ **Coach**: Record correct responses by placing a check mark next to the correctly answered component on the Worksheet Data Recording Sheet. Place completed work in the student's daily folder.

❑ **Assessment**: Set the timer for one minute. The student should read the passage aloud to the teacher. Instruct the student to stop when the timer buzzes. Again, set the timer for one minute and instruct the student to tell the teacher what the passage was about. The teacher should mark the number of words from the passage that the student uses during the retell.

❑ **Coach**: Complete the Assessment Data Recording Sheet.

Improving Comprehension Using Story Maps:
Sample Worksheet

Student: __Kalip__   Grade: __6__

Teacher: __Mr. Puffinberger__   Date: __December 13__

Title of Story: ___Harry Potter and the Sorcerer's Stone: Chapter 1___

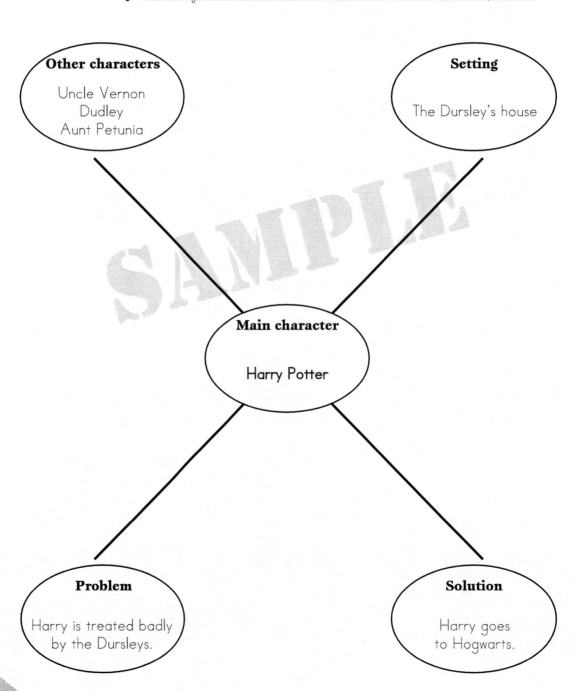

Other characters

Uncle Vernon
Dudley
Aunt Petunia

Setting

The Dursley's house

Main character

Harry Potter

Problem

Harry is treated badly
by the Dursleys.

Solution

Harry goes
to Hogwarts.

Improving Comprehension Using Story Maps: Worksheet

Student: _____   Grade: _____

Teacher: _____   Date: _____

Title of Story: _____

```
  ( Other characters )                    ( Setting )


                      ( Main character )


  ( Problem )                              ( Solution )
```

Improving Comprehension Using Story Maps:
Worksheet Data Recording Sheet

Student: _____   Grade: _____

Teacher: _____   Date begun: _____

Date ended: _____

Scoring instructions: For each story read and Worksheet completed, place a check mark along with the day's date in the column next to the correctly answered component.

Story components	Date					
1. Main character						
2. Main character(s)						
3. Other characters						
4. Setting						
5. Problem						
6. Solution						

Notes:

Improving Comprehension Using Story Retell

Objective: This tactic is designed to improve students' reading comprehension by "retelling" a story through answering questions.

Materials: Daily folder, Worksheet, Rating Scale, reading passages (classroom reading textbooks may be used), pencil, timer, and two Data Recording Sheets as described on the Coach Card.

 Requires approximately **20 minutes** each day (one to two days per week).

Preparation: Make copies of tactic reproducibles and gather remaining tactic materials. Make copies of selected reading passages, and make one copy of the Worksheet to be used with each reading passage. Choose stories from the student's independent and/or instructional reading level (teacher should base levels on formal/informal testing results).

Coach Card

❑ Get materials. Go to an assigned work area. Find the day's reading passage.

❑ **Coach**: Find the day's Worksheet.

❑ **Coach**: Write the student's name, teacher name, grade, and date on the Worksheet.

❑ **Student**: Read the reading passage silently.

❑ **Coach**: Read each question on the Worksheet to the student.

❑ **Student**: Respond orally to each question.

❑ **Coach**: Write the answer given to each question on the Worksheet.

❑ **Coach**: Score the Worksheet by using the Rating Scale, which follows.

❑ **Coach**: Record correct responses on the Worksheet Data Recording Sheet. Place completed work in the student's daily folder. Correct mistakes.

❑ **Assessment**: Set the timer for one minute. The student should read the passage aloud to the teacher. Instruct the student to stop when the timer buzzes. Instruct the student to tell the teacher what the passage was about, again setting the timer for one minute. Using the Data Recording Sheet (Assessment Component) found at the back of this chapter, the teacher should mark the number of words from the passage that the student uses during the retell.

❑ **Coach**: On the Assessment Data Recording Sheet, document the number of words from the passage that the student uses during the retell.

Improving Comprehension Using Story Retell: Worksheet

Student: _____   Grade: _____

Teacher: _____   Date: _____

Title of Story: _____

1. Who is the main character? _____

   _____

2. What is the main character like? _____

   _____

3. Is there another important character in the story? Who? _____

   _____

4. Where does the story take place? _____

   _____

5. What is the main character's problem? _____

   _____

6. How does the main character try to solve his/her problem? _____

   _____

   _____

7. What is the twist/complication in the story? _____

   _____

8. How is the problem solved or not solved _____

   _____

9. What is the theme or lesson of the story? _____

   _____

Improving Comprehension Using Story Retell: Sample Worksheet

Student: _Meg_   Grade: _6_

Teacher: _Ms. McAndrews_   Date: _March 12_

Title of Story: _Harry Potter and the Sorcerer's Stone: Chapter 1_

1. Who is the main character? _The main character is Harry Potter_

2. What is the main character like? _Harry is a male wizard. He is very smart and interested in wizards._

3. Is there another important character in the story? Who? _Uncle Dursley is an important character in Chapter 1._

4. What is this person like? _Uncle Dursley is a mean man who is happiest when Harry is miserable. He is very rude to Harry and treats him badly._

5. Where does the story take place? _The setting of Chapter 1 is the Dursleys' house._

6. What is the main character's problem? _Harry's parents died and he must stay with his aunt, uncle, and cousin. The Dursleys do not like Harry and they treat him badly._

7. How does the main character try to solve his/her problem? _Harry tries to keep his distance from the Dursleys. When he is around them, he tries to be quiet so he won't bring attention to himself._

8. What is the twist/complication in the story? _Harry is a wizard and the Dursleys are muggles (not wizards)._

9. How is the problem solved or not solved _Harry goes away to attend school at Hogwarts._

10. What is the theme or lesson of the story? _There are people in life whom we do not get along with. When this happens, we should make the best of it or stay away from them._

Improving Comprehension Using Story Retell: Data Recording Sheet (Worksheet)

Student: _____   Grade: _____

Teacher: _____   Date begun: _____

Date ended: _____

Scoring instructions: Write a (+) for correct answers and a (/) for incorrect answers.

Date	Name of story	Main character	Description of main character	Supporting characters	Setting	Problem	Solution	Lesson learned

Notes:

Improving Comprehension Using Main Idea Maps

Objective: This tactic is designed to improve recognition of main idea with the use of a graphic organizer.

Materials: Daily folder, overheads of reading passages, Worksheet, timer, and two Data Recording Sheets as described on the Coach Card.

 Requires approximately **30 minutes** each day (one to two times per week).

Preparation: Make copies of tactic reproducibles and gather tactic materials. Review tactic with a student or a group of students. Prepare overheads of selected reading passages (expository or reading textbooks from the classroom may be used). Prepare daily folders with reading passages and Main Idea Map Worksheet.

Note: This tactic can be implemented with an individual or a group of students.

Coach Card

❏ Get materials. Go to assigned work area. Find the day's reading passage and Worksheet. Using overheads of the reading passage and the Worksheet, complete the following steps:

❏ **Model**: Read the first paragraph of the reading passage.

❏ **Model**: Write the main idea of the paragraph on the Worksheet.

❏ **Model**: Write the key points of the paragraph under the main idea.

❏ **Model**: Read the second paragraph of the reading passage.

❏ **Model**: Write the main idea of the paragraph on the Worksheet.

❏ **Model**: Write the key points of the paragraph under the main idea.

❏ **Model**: Continue the process through the reading passage.

❏ **Coach**: Once student completes tactic, score and review tactic with student. Correct any mistakes.

❏ **Coach**: Record correct responses by placing a check mark next to the component answered correctly on the Worksheet Data Recording Sheet. Place completed work in the student's daily folder.

❏ **Assessment**: Set the timer for one minute. The student should read the passage aloud to the teacher. Instruct the student to stop when the timer buzzes. Instruct the student to tell the teacher what the passage was about, again setting the timer for one minute. Using the Data Recording Sheet (Assessment Component) found at the back of this chapter, the teacher should mark the number of words from the passage that the student uses during the retell.

❏ **Coach**: On the Assessment Data Recording Sheet, document the number of words from the passage that the student uses during the retell.

Improving Comprehension Using Main Idea Maps: Worksheet

Student: _____ Grade: _____

Teacher: _____ Date: _____

Main idea 1:	**Main idea 2:**
_____	_____
Key point 1: _____	Key point 1: _____
_____	_____
Key point 2: _____	Key point 2: _____
_____	_____
Key point 3: _____	Key point 3: _____
_____	_____

Title:

_____

_____

Main idea 3:	**Main idea 4:**
_____	_____
Key point 1: _____	Key point 1: _____
_____	_____
Key point 2: _____	Key point 2: _____
_____	_____
Key point 3: _____	Key point 3: _____
_____	_____

Improving Comprehension Using Main Idea Maps: Data Recording Sheet (Worksheet)

Student: _____   Grade: _____

Teacher: _____   Date begun: _____

Date ended: _____

Scoring instructions: Place a check mark in each column answered correctly and record the total.

Date	Paragraph number	Main idea number	Key point 1	Key point 2	Key point 3	Total

Notes:

Improving Comprehension Using TELLS

Objective: This tactic is designed to improve comprehension of narrative structure.

Materials: Daily folder, grade-appropriate narrative text passages, Worksheet, timer, and two Data Recording Sheets as described on the Coach Card.

Preparation: Make copies of tactic reproducibles and gather remaining tactic materials. Make copies of selected grade-appropriate narrative text passages.

 Requires approximately **30 minutes** each day (one to two times per week).

Coach Card

- ❏ Get materials. Go to an assigned work area. Take out the day's narrative text passage and the Worksheet.

- ❏ **Model**: **T**—Study the story TITLES (look through the text).

- ❏ **Model**: **E**—EXAMINE and skim pages for clues about the text. Write clues on the worksheet.

- ❏ **Model**: **L**—LOOK for important words. **L**—LOOK for difficult words. Write these words on the worksheet.

- ❏ **Model**: **S**—Think about the story SETTING. Write the setting on the Worksheet.

- ❏ **Coach**: Review completed Worksheet with the student. Correct any mistakes. Document results on Worksheet Data Recording Sheet.

- ❏ **Assessment**: Set the timer for one minute. The student should read the passage aloud to the teacher. Instruct the student to stop when the timer buzzes. Instruct the student to tell the teacher what the passage was about, again setting the timer for one minute. Using the Data Recording Sheet (Assessment Component) found at the back of this chapter, the teacher should mark the number of words from the passage that the student uses during the retell.

- ❏ **Coach**: Record results on the Data Recording Sheet.

Improving Comprehension Using TELLS: Worksheet

Student: _____   Grade: _____

Teacher: _____   Date: _____

Story Titles

_____

_____

_____

_____

Clues

_____

_____

_____

_____

Important and/or Difficult Words

_____

_____

_____

_____

Story Setting

_____

_____

_____

_____

Improving Comprehension Using TELLS:
Data Recording Sheet (Worksheet)

Student: _____   Grade: _____

Teacher: _____   Date begun: _____

Date ended: _____

Scoring instructions: Write a (+) for correct answers and a (/) for incorrect answers.

Date	Name of story	Main character	Description of main character	Supporting characters	Setting	Problem	Solution	Lesson learned

Notes:

Improving Vocabulary Using IT FITS

Objective: As a result of this tactic, students will better remember unfamiliar vocabulary words, improving their reading comprehension.

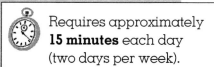

Requires approximately **15 minutes** each day (two days per week).

Materials: Daily folder, paper, pencil, index cards, grade-appropriate reading material (narratives and/or expository textbooks may be used), timer, dictionary, scoring rubric, and two Data Recording Sheets as described on the Coach Card.

Preparation: Choose grade-appropriate reading materials for use with this tactic. Make copies of coach card and Data Recording Sheet. Create a student folder to hold work.

Coach Card

- ❑ Get materials. Go to an assigned work area.

- ❑ Have the student read the passage aloud. When the reader comes upon a word he/she doesn't know, complete the following steps:

- ❑ **Model**: **I**—IDENTIFY the term. (Write the term on an index card.)

- ❑ **Model**: **T**—TELL the definition. (Look up definition in the dictionary and write the definition on the index card.)

- ❑ **Model**: **F**—FIND a key word you know that will help you to remember the vocabulary word. (Write the word on the card.)

- ❑ **Model**: **I**—IMAGINE and **T**—THINK. (Draw a picture on the index card to help remember the relationship between the definition and key word.)

- ❑ **Model**: **S**—STUDY. (Study the developed index card until you know the definition.)

- ❑ **Coach**: Present the student with a reading passage and index card. Instruct the student to complete the Coach Card for the IT FITS tactic without assistance. When timer buzzes, ask the student to stop.

- ❑ **Coach**: Evaluate each index card using the scoring rubric included on the Worksheet Data Recording Sheet.

- ❑ **Assessment**: Set the timer for one minute. The student should read the passage aloud to the teacher. Instruct the student to stop when the timer buzzes. Instruct the student to tell the teacher what the passage was about, again setting the timer for one minute. Using the Data Recording Sheet (Assessment Component) found at the back of this chapter, the teacher should mark the number of words from the passage that the student uses during the retell.

- ❑ **Coach**: On the Assessment Data Recording Sheet, document the number of words from the passage that the student uses during the retell.

Improving Vocabulary Using IT FITS:
Data Recording Sheet (Worksheet)

Student: _____   Grade: _____

Teacher: _____   Date begun: _____

                                             Date ended: _____

Instructions:

1. Is the vocabulary word definition correct? (5 points)

2. Does the key word have the same meaning as the vocabulary word? (5 points)

3. Does the picture properly represent the vocabulary word? (5 points)

Date	Vocabulary word definition	Key word	Picture	Total points

Notes:

Improving Vocabulary Using IT FITS: Sample Reading Passage

Land Biomes

Earth's Biomes

Biomes are unique, very specialized ecosystems that only exist in certain parts of the world. These ecosystems are defined by the environment. Things like temperature, rainfall, and altitude all determine what type of life a biome can support. Types of biomes include tropical rain forest, desert, tundra, and savanna.

Flesch-Kincaid Grade Level: 10.3

Data Recording Sheet (Assessment Component)

Student: _____ Grade: _____

Teacher: _____ Date begun: _____

Date ended: _____

Date: _____ Passage name: _____

Number of words from passage used in retell _____

1	2	3	4	5	6	7	8	9	10	11	12	13	14	15	16	17	18	19	20
21	22	23	24	25	26	27	28	29	30	31	32	33	34	35	36	37	38	39	40
41	42	43	44	45	46	47	48	49	50	51	52	53	54	55	56	57	58	59	60
61	62	63	64	65	66	67	68	69	70	71	72	73	74	75	76	77	78	79	80

Date: _____ Passage name: _____

Number of words from passage used in retell _____

1	2	3	4	5	6	7	8	9	10	11	12	13	14	15	16	17	18	19	20
21	22	23	24	25	26	27	28	29	30	31	32	33	34	35	36	37	38	39	40
41	42	43	44	45	46	47	48	49	50	51	52	53	54	55	56	57	58	59	60
61	62	63	64	65	66	67	68	69	70	71	72	73	74	75	76	77	78	79	80

Date: _____ Passage name: _____

Number of words from passage used in retell _____

1	2	3	4	5	6	7	8	9	10	11	12	13	14	15	16	17	18	19	20
21	22	23	24	25	26	27	28	29	30	31	32	33	34	35	36	37	38	39	40
41	42	43	44	45	46	47	48	49	50	51	52	53	54	55	56	57	58	59	60
61	62	63	64	65	66	67	68	69	70	71	72	73	74	75	76	77	78	79	80

2

Spelling Tactics

Never trust a man that spells a word the same way twice.

—Mark Twain

Proficient spelling ability is dependent on the speller's sensitivity to letter patterns (Adams, 1990). What differentiates good spellers from poor spellers is that good spellers possess well-developed phonological processing skills that not only make them aware of the sounds in words but also support the learning of letter patterns in words (Lennox & Siegel, 1998; Moats, 1995). Good spellers possess an orthographic memory, which is a more defined memory than visual memory specific to remembering letter patterns and symbols. Good spellers know how sounds are represented in language and how words should look in print (Adams, 1990). Contrary to beliefs, research has shown that good and poor spellers do not differ greatly in their visual memory abilities (Lennox & Siegel, 1996).

Good spellers are frequently good readers because good spellers have the very skills necessary for decoding. Although both reading and spelling require phonological and orthographic knowledge, they are not merely inverse operations (Frith, 1990). Encoding, or sound-to-spelling translations, is less dependable than decoding, which involves spelling-to-sound translations (Adams, 1990). Moreover, decoding requires recognition of words, whereas spelling requires complete, accurate recall of letter patterns and words (Frith & Frith, 1980; Fulk & Stormont-Spurgin, 1995). It is unusual to find a good speller who is a poor reader. It is possible, however, for students to be reasonably good readers but poor spellers (Moats, 1995).

Because many speech sounds in English have multiple spellings, making a correct choice can be confusing for the speller. The speller's only verification of a correct spelling is to compare the spelled word with a word held in memory. If the word is not held in memory or if the speller has a poor memory for letters and words, it is difficult for the speller to verify that the spelling choice is correct. Spelling requires an awareness of and precise memory for letter patterns and words that reading does not require.

The spelling tactics in this chapter incorporate visual, auditory, and kinesthetic learning styles. The tactics involve active student participation , moving away from the typical rote-memory techniques used when teaching spelling. The beginning tactics in the chapter use a more hands-on approach to learning spelling words, using letter tiles, scrambled letters, read and draw, glitter, sandpaper, stamp letters, newspaper cut outs, and sand writing. The remaining spelling tactics involve pencil and paper techniques to teaching spelling, including word searches, linking letters, modified cloze, and add-a-word techniques. The final two tactics "Add a Word" and "Write–Say Method" involve a combination of written, spoken, and auditory techniques. The tactics are presented in a way in which more tangible, hands-on approaches are presented first, followed by more advanced approaches of writing. The vast array of creative tactics presented in this chapter will equip students with a system to become functional spellers and to make spelling fun.

Improving Skills Using Letter Tiles

Objective: This tactic is designed to improve spelling and written communication.

Materials: Daily folder, weekly spelling word list (10 words), magnetic letters or letter tiles, timer, paper, pencil, and Data Recording Sheet.

 Requires approximately **10 minutes** (two times per week).

Preparation: Make copies of tactic reproducibles and gather remaining tactic materials. Make copies of the selected grade-appropriate spelling word list (10 words). Teacher may purchase letter tiles or create them by making a copy of the Letter Tiles sheet.

Coach Card

- ❏ Get materials. Go to an assigned work area.
- ❏ **Coach**: Find the weekly spelling word list. Place the letter tiles (entire alphabet) randomly on the table.
- ❏ **Coach**: Pronounce the first word of the list aloud.
- ❏ **Student**: Choose the appropriate letter tiles to spell the pronounced word.
- ❏ **Student**: Place the letter tiles in the appropriate order to spell the pronounced word.
- ❏ **Coach**: Pronounce the second word aloud and have the student choose tiles and place them in the appropriate order. If a word is misspelled, the coach should make corrections and instruct the student to try again. Continue until all spelling words have been pronounced and spelled with the letter tiles.
- ❏ **Assessment**: Set the timer for three minutes. Have the student use the letter tiles to spell and then pronounce as many words as possible without assistance during the three-minute period. When the timer buzzes, ask the student to stop.
- ❏ **Coach**: Record the responses on the Data Recording Sheet.

Improving Skills Using Letter Tiles: Letter Tiles

a	b	c	d
e	f	g	h
i	j	k	l
m	n	o	p
q	r	s	t
u	v	w	x
y	z		

Improving Skills Using Letter Tiles:
Data Recording Sheet

Student: _____   Grade: _____

Teacher: _____   Date: _____

Scoring instructions: Write each word on the weekly spelling word list in the left column of the chart. Place a (+) in the column beside the words that are spelled correctly. Place a (/) in the column beside the words spelled incorrectly. Total the number of correct and incorrect responses.

Weekly spelling words	Words spelled correctly (+) or incorrectly (/)

Total number of words spelled correctly: _____

Total number of words spelled incorrectly: _____

Notes:

Improving Skills Using Scrambled Words

Objective: This tactic is designed to improve spelling and written communication.

Materials: Daily folder, weekly spelling word list, magnetic letters or letter tiles, timer, paper, pencil, and Data Recording Sheet.

 Requires approximately **10 minutes** (one to two times per week).

Preparation: Make copies of tactic reproducibles and gather remaining tactic materials. Make copies of the selected grade-appropriate spelling word list (10 words). Teacher may purchase letter tiles or create them by making a copy of the Letter Tiles sheet.

Coach Card

- ❑ Get materials and go to an assigned work area.

- ❑ **Coach**: Find the weekly spelling word list. Scramble the letter tiles of each word randomly on the table. (Scramble tiles for just one word at a time).

- ❑ **Coach**: Pronounce the first word on the list aloud.

- ❑ **Student**: Place the letter tiles in the appropriate order to spell the pronounced word.

- ❑ **Coach**: Pronounce the second word aloud and have the student place the scrambled tiles in the appropriate order. If a word is misspelled, the teacher or peer helper should make corrections and instruct the student to try again. Continue until all spelling words have been pronounced and spelled with the letter tiles.

- ❑ **Assessment**: Set the timer for three minutes. Scramble the letter tiles representing words from the spelling word list. Have the student use the scrambled letter tiles to spell as many words as possible without assistance during the three-minute period. When the timer buzzes, ask the student to stop.

- ❑ **Coach**: Record results on the Data Recording Sheet.

Improving Skills Using Scrambled Words: Letter Tiles

a	b	c	d
e	f	g	h
i	j	k	l
m	n	o	p
q	r	s	t
u	v	w	x
y	z		

Improving Skills Using Scrambled Words:
Data Recording Sheet

Student: _____   Grade: _____

Teacher: _____   Date: _____

Scoring instructions: Write each word on the weekly spelling word list in the left column of the chart. Place a (+) in the column beside the words that are spelled correctly. Place a (/) in the column beside the words spelled incorrectly. Total the number of correct and incorrect responses.

Weekly spelling words	Words spelled correctly (+) or incorrectly (/)

Total number of words spelled correctly: _____

Total number of words spelled incorrectly: _____

Notes:

Improving Skills Using Read and Draw

Objective: This tactic is designed to improve spelling and written communication.

Materials: Daily folder, weekly spelling word list, timer, colored pencils, paper, pencil, and Data Recording Sheet.

Preparation: Make copies of tactic reproducibles and gather remaining tactic materials. Make copies of selected grade-appropriate spelling word list (10 words).

 Requires approximately **10 minutes** (one to two times per week).

Coach Card

- ❑ Get materials. Go to an assigned work area. Find the weekly spelling word list.
- ❑ **Coach**: Instruct the student to read through the spelling word list aloud.
- ❑ **Student**: Pronounce the first word of the list aloud.
- ❑ **Student**: Draw a picture/symbol representing the word.
- ❑ **Student**: Pronounce the second word of the list aloud.
- ❑ **Student**: Draw a picture/symbol representing the word. Continue until all spelling words have been pronounced and pictures have been drawn.
- ❑ **Assessment**: Instruct the student to read each word aloud. Time for one minute.
- ❑ **Coach**: Record results on the Data Recording Sheet.

Improving Skills Using Read and Draw:
Data Recording Sheet

Student: _____   Grade: _____

Teacher: _____   Date: _____

Scoring instructions: Write each word on the weekly spelling word list in the left column of the chart. Place a (+) in the column beside the words that are pronounced correctly. Place a (/) in the column beside the words pronounced incorrectly. Total the number of correct and incorrect responses.

Weekly spelling words	Words spelled correctly (+) or incorrectly (/)

Total number of words spelled correctly: _____

Total number of words spelled incorrectly: _____

Notes:

Improving Skills Using Glitter Writing

Objective: This tactic is designed to improve visualization of spelling words. This tactic integrates visual and tactile learning strategies.

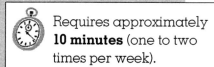

Requires approximately **10 minutes** (one to two times per week).

Materials: Daily folder, weekly spelling word list, glue stick, paper, glitter, timer, index cards, markers, and Data Recording Sheet.

Preparation: Make copies of tactic reproducibles and gather remaining tactic materials. Make copies of selected spelling word list to use during this tactic (10 spelling words). Using markers, write one word on each index card to form flash cards. Place paper, glue, and glitter in a container for easy access.

Coach Card

- ❏ Get materials. Go to an assigned work area. Arrange materials; find flash cards.
- ❏ **Coach**: Hold up the first flash card and say the word written on it.
- ❏ **Student**: Using the glue stick, write the word on your paper and cover it with glitter.
- ❏ **Student**: Say the word. And then spell the word.
- ❏ **Coach**: Check for accuracy and encourage the student.
- ❏ **Coach**: Hold up the second flash card and say the word.
- ❏ **Student**: Using the glue stick, write the word on your paper and cover it with glitter.
- ❏ **Student**: Say the word. And then spell the word
- ❏ **Coach**: Check for accuracy and encourage the student. Continue the process, presenting the remaining flash cards.
- ❏ **Assessment**: Set the timer for three minutes. Assess how well the student can spell the words on each flash card. Say the word on the flash card. Have the student spell the word aloud in five seconds or less. If the student cannot spell the word in the time allotment, put the flash card in the missed stack. If the student can spell the word correctly in the time allowed, put the flash card in the "Got it" stack. Next, dictate each word aloud and have the student write each word on a sheet of paper. Enter the scores on the Data Recording Sheet. When the timer buzzes, ask the student to stop.
- ❏ **Coach**: Record results on the Data Recording Sheet.

Improving Skills Using Glitter Writing:
Data Recording Sheet

Student: _____ Grade: _____

Teacher: _____ Date: _____

Scoring instructions: Place a (+) in the spelling and pronunciation columns if answered correctly. Place a (/) in the columns if answered incorrectly.

Weekly spelling words	Spelling aloud	Written words

Total number of words spelled correctly: _____ incorrectly: _____

Total number of words pronounced correctly: _____ incorrectly: _____

Notes:

Improving Skills Using Sandpaper Cut Outs

Objective: This tactic is designed to improve visualization of spelling words. This tactic integrates visual and tactile learning strategies.

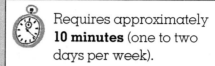 Requires approximately **10 minutes** (one to two days per week).

Materials: Daily folder, weekly spelling word list (5–10 words), sheets of sandpaper, alphabet cut outs, large (8½ x 11) envelope, timer, and Data Recording Sheet.

Preparation: Make copies of tactic reproducibles and gather remaining tactic materials. Make copies of selected weekly spelling word list. Using alphabet letter cut outs and sheets of sandpaper, cut out sandpaper letters of the alphabet.

Coach Card

❑ Get materials. Go to an assigned work area.

❑ **Coach**: Take out the weekly spelling word list and the sandpaper letter cut outs.

❑ **Coach**: Read the first word on the spelling list.

❑ **Student**: Tell the student to spell out the word using the sandpaper letter cut outs. Model one word., spell out the word.

❑ **Student**: Next, tell the student to trace each letter in the word made from the sandpaper letter cut outs and say each letter as he/she is tracing it.

❑ **Student**: When the student has finished spelling the word, tell him or her to say the word.

❑ **Coach**: Continue the process through the remainder of the spelling word list.

❑ **Assessment**: Set the timer for three minutes. Assess how well the student can spell the words that were practiced. Say each word, and have the student spell the word aloud in five seconds or less. Record the score on the Data Recording Sheet. Next, dictate each word aloud and have the student write each word on a sheet of paper. When the timer buzzes, ask the student to stop. Enter the scores on the Data Recording Sheet.

❑ **Coach**: Record results on the Data Recording Sheet.

Improving Skills Using Sandpaper Cut Outs:
Data Recording Sheet

Student: _____ Grade: _____

Teacher: _____ Date: _____

Scoring instructions: Place a (+) in the spelling and pronunciation columns if the answer is correct. Place a (/) in the columns if the answer is incorrect.

Weekly spelling words	Spelling	Pronunciation

Total number of words spelled correctly: _____ incorrectly: _____

Total number of words pronounced correctly: _____ incorrectly: _____

Notes:

Improving Skills Using Alphabet Stamps

Objective: This tactic is designed to improve visualization of spelling words.

Materials: Daily folder, weekly spelling word list (10 words), ink pad, alphabet stamps, paper, timer, and Data Recording Sheet.

Preparation: Make copies of tactic reproducibles and gather remaining tactic materials. Make copies of selected weekly spelling word list.

 Requires approximately **10 minutes** each day (one to two days per week).

Coach Card

- ❑ Get materials. Go to an assigned work area. Find the weekly spelling word list.

- ❑ **Student**: Read each word on the list aloud.

- ❑ **Coach**: Check for accuracy and provide feedback.

- ❑ **Coach**: After the student completes a first read of all the words on the spelling word list, instruct the student to read aloud the first word on the list.

- ❑ **Coach**: Cover the first word and instruct the student to choose appropriate stamps to spell the word.

- ❑ **Student**: Stamp the word on your paper.

- ❑ **Coach**: Instruct the student to read the second word on the list.

- ❑ **Coach**: Cover the word and instruct the student to choose appropriate stamps to spell the word.

- ❑ **Student**: Stamp the word on your paper.

- ❑ **Coach**: Continue the process until all the words on the spelling word list have been stamped out.

- ❑ **Assessment**: Set the timer for three minutes. Assess how well the student can spell the words that were practiced. Say each word, and have the student spell the word aloud in five seconds or less. Record the score on the Data Recording Sheet. Next, dictate each word aloud and have the student write each word on a sheet of paper. When the timer buzzes, ask the student to stop. Enter the scores on the Data Recording Sheet.

- ❑ **Coach**: Record results on the Data Recording Sheet.

Improving Skills Using Alphabet Stamps:
Data Recording Sheet

Student: _____   Grade: _____

Teacher: _____   Date: _____

Scoring instructions: Place a (+) in the spelling and pronunciation columns if answered correctly. Place a (/) in the columns if answered incorrectly.

Weekly spelling words	Spelling	Pronunciation

Total number of words spelled correctly: _____ incorrectly: _____

Total number of words pronounced correctly: _____ incorrectly: _____

Notes:

Improving Skills Using Newspaper Cut Outs

Objective: This tactic is designed to improve visualization of spelling words and enhance fine motor skills.

Materials: Daily folder, weekly spelling word list (ten words), magazines or newspapers, glue, scissors, timer, pencil, and Data Recording Sheet.

Preparation: Make copies of tactic reproducibles and gather remaining tactic materials. Make copies of selected weekly spelling word list.

 Requires approximately **20 minutes** each day (one to two times per week).

Coach Card

- ❑ Get materials. Go to an assigned work area.

- ❑ **Coach**: Using the spelling word list, pronounce first word aloud.

- ❑ **Student**: Search through newspapers/magazines to find the word or letters to form the pronounced word.

- ❑ **Student**: Cut out the word or letters to form the word.

- ❑ **Student**: Glue the word or letter cut outs to a sheet of paper.

- ❑ **Coach**: Using the spelling word list, pronounce the second word aloud.

- ❑ **Student**: Search through newspapers/magazines to find the word or letters to form the pronounced word.

- ❑ **Student**: Cut out the word or letters to form the word.

- ❑ **Student**: Glue the word or letter cut outs to a sheet of paper.

- ❑ **Coach**: Continue the process until all spelling words are pronounced and the student's sheet is complete.

- ❑ **Assessment**: Set the timer for three minutes. Assess how well the student can spell the words that were practiced. Say each word, and have the student spell the word aloud in five seconds or less. Record the score on the Data Recording Sheet. Next, dictate each word aloud and have the student write each word on a sheet of paper. When the timer buzzes, ask the student to stop. Enter the scores on the Data Recording Sheet.

- ❑ **Coach**: Record results on the Data Recording Sheet.

Improving Skills Using Newspaper Cut-Outs: Data Recording Sheet

Student: _____ Grade: _____

Teacher: _____ Date: _____

Scoring instructions: Place a (+) in second column if the word is spelled correctly. Place a (/) in the second column if the word is spelled incorrectly.

Weekly spelling words	Words spelled correctly (+) or incorrectly (/)

Total number of words spelled correctly: _____ incorrectly: _____

Total number of words pronounced correctly: _____ incorrectly: _____

Notes:

Improving Skills Using Sand Writing

Objective: This tactic is designed to improve visualization of spelling words. This tactic integrates visual and tactile learning strategies.

 Requires approximately **10 minutes** each day (one to two times per week).

Materials: Daily folder, weekly spelling word list (10 words), small box filled with sand, index cards, markers, timer, and Data Recording Sheet.

Preparation: Make copies of tactic reproducibles and gather remaining tactic materials. Using words from the weekly spelling word list, write one word on each index card to form flash cards. Fill small box with sand.

Coach Card

- ❑ Get materials. Go to an assigned work area.
- ❑ **Coach**: Take out the weekly spelling word list and the sand.
- ❑ **Coach**: Read the first word on the spelling list.
- ❑ **Student**: Tell the student to spell out the word in the sand. Model one word; spell out the word.
- ❑ **Student**: Next, tell the student to trace each letter in the word in the sand, and to say each letter as he/she is tracing it.
- ❑ **Student**: When the student has finished spelling the word, tell him or her to say the word.
- ❑ **Coach**: Continue the process through the remainder of the spelling word list.
- ❑ **Assessment**: Set the timer for three minutes. Assess how well the student can spell the words that were practiced. Say each word, and have the student spell the word aloud in five seconds or less. Record the score on the Data Recording Sheet. Next, dictate each word aloud and have the student write each word on a sheet of paper. When the timer buzzes, ask the student to stop. Enter the scores on the Data Recording Sheet.
- ❑ **Coach**: Record results on the Data Recording Sheet.

Improving Skills Using Sand Writing:
Data Recording Sheet

Student: _____ Grade: _____

Teacher: _____ Date: _____

Scoring instructions: Place a (+) in the spelling and pronunciation columns if answered correctly. Place a (/) in the columns if answered incorrectly.

Weekly spelling words	Spelling	Pronunciation

Total number of words spelled correctly: _____ incorrectly: _____

Total number of words pronounced correctly: _____ incorrectly: _____

Notes:

Improving Skills Using Word Searches

Objective: This tactic reinforces sequencing of letters, enhances memory, and allows students to practice spelling skills.

 Requires approximately **15 minutes** each day (one to two times per week).

Materials: Daily folder, weekly spelling word list (10 words), worksheet (teacher-created), paper, pencil, highlighter, timer, and Data Recording Sheet.

Preparation: Make copies of tactic reproducibles and gather remaining tactic materials. Choose words from the weekly spelling word list to create and make copies of a word search worksheet (see Sample Worksheet).

Coach Card

- ❑ Get materials. Go to an assigned work area. Take out the day's Worksheet.

- ❑ Write names, grade, and date on the Worksheet.

- ❑ **Coach**: Instruct the student to read the "word list" section of the Sample Worksheet.

- ❑ **Student**: Search for words from the word list that are hidden in the "word search" section of the Worksheet.

- ❑ **Student**: Using a highlighter, mark the hidden words you find.

- ❑ **Student**: Continue until all the words in the word list have been highlighted.

- ❑ **Assessment**: Set the timer for three minutes. Have the student find and highlight as many words as possible without assistance during the three-minute period. When the timer buzzes, ask the student to stop.

- ❑ **Coach**: Record results on the Data Recording Sheet.

Improving Skills Using Word Searches:
Sample Worksheet

Word List

car

shark

dog

cat

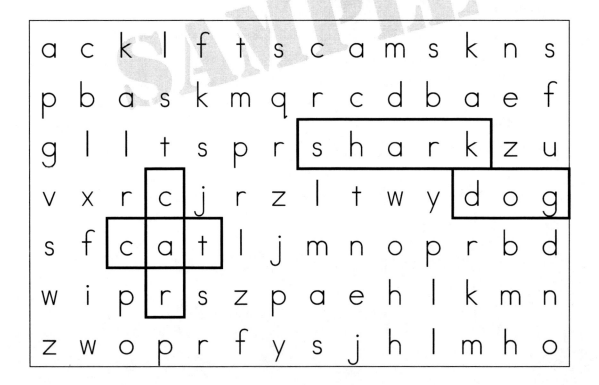

Chapter 2 • *Tactics for Boosting Academic Achievement*

Improving Skills Using Word Searches

Improving Skills Using Word Searches:
Data Recording Sheet

Student: _____   Grade: _____

Teacher: _____   Date: _____

Scoring instructions: Place a (+) in second column if the word is found. Place a (/) in the second column if the word is not found.

Weekly spelling words	Words spelled correctly (+) or incorrectly (/)
_____	
_____	
_____	
_____	
_____	
_____	
_____	
_____	
_____	
_____	

Total number of words spelled correctly: _____   incorrectly: _____

Total number of words pronounced correctly: _____   incorrectly: _____

Notes:

Improving Skills Using Link Letters

Objective: This tactic is designed to improve visualization of spelling words.

Materials: Daily folder, weekly spelling word list, envelope to hold puzzle pieces, heavy cardboard, paper or oaktag, markers, timer, and Data Recording Sheet.

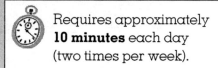

Requires approximately **10 minutes** each day (two times per week).

Preparation: Make copies of tactic reproducibles and gather remaining tactic materials. Make copies of the weekly spelling word list (10 words) and, using markers, write the spelling words on heavy paper. Separate each word by cutting it into two or more pieces (to form puzzle pieces).

Coach Card

❑ Get materials. Go to an assigned work area. Take the weekly spelling word list and puzzle pieces out of the envelope.

❑ **Coach**: Spread the pieces out on the table (letters facing up).

❑ **Student**: Link the word sections together to form a word from the spelling word list.

❑ **Student**: Continue the process until all the word sections are linked and all the words on the spelling word list are formed.

❑ **Assessment**: Set the timer for three minutes. Assess how well the student can spell the words that were practiced. Say each word, and have the student spell the word aloud in five seconds or less. Record the score on the Data Recording Sheet. Next, dictate each word aloud and have the student write each word on a sheet of paper. When the timer buzzes, ask the student to stop. Enter the scores on the Data Recording Sheet.

❑ **Coach**: Record results on the Data Recording Sheet.

Improving Skills Using Link Letters:
Data Recording Sheet

Student: _____ Grade: _____

Teacher: _____ Date: _____

Scoring instructions: Place a (+) in the spelling and pronunciation columns if the answer is correct. Place a (/) in the columns if the answer is incorrect.

Weekly spelling words	Spelling	Pronunciation

Total number of words spelled correctly: _____ incorrectly: _____

Total number of words pronounced correctly: _____ incorrectly: _____

Notes:

Improving Skills Using Modified Cloze

Objective: This tactic reinforces sequencing of letters, enhances memory, and allows students to practice spelling skills.

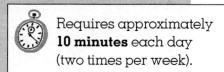

Requires approximately **10 minutes** each day (two times per week).

Materials: Daily folder, weekly spelling word list, modified cloze worksheet (teacher-created), paper, pencil, timer, and Data Recording Sheet.

Preparation: Make copies of tactic reproducibles and gather remaining tactic materials. Choose a weekly spelling word list (10 words). Using words from this list, design and create a modified cloze worksheet consisting of selected spelling words and fill-in-the-blank sentences (see Sample Worksheet).

Coach Card

- ❑ Get materials. Go to an assigned work area. Take out the modified cloze worksheet. Write names, grade, and date on the worksheet.

- ❑ **Coach**: Instruct the student to read the "word list" section aloud. Check for accuracy and provide feedback to the student.

- ❑ **Student**: Read each sentence in the "cloze sentence" section of the worksheet.

- ❑ **Student**: Choose the appropriate word from the word list to complete the first cloze sentence.

- ❑ **Student**: Write the appropriate word in the blank space provided.

- ❑ **Coach**: Continue the process until all the sentences on the worksheet are complete.

- ❑ **Assessment**: Set the timer for three minutes. Have the student complete as many cloze sentences on the worksheet as possible and without assistance during the three-minute period. When the timer buzzes, ask the student to stop.

- ❑ **Coach**: Record results on the Data Recording Sheet.

Improving Skills Using Modified Cloze: Sample Worksheet

Student: _____   Grade: _____

Teacher: _____   Date: _____

Word List

car

dog

sun

girl

Cloze Sentences

Directions: Choose the appropriate word from the word list above to complete each sentence. Write your answers in the blanks.

1. The _____ was shining brightly.

2. The man drove the _____ fast.

3. The _____ barked loudly.

4. There is a new _____ in town.

Improving Skills Using Modified Cloze:
Data Recording Sheet

Student: _____   Grade: _____

Teacher: _____   Date: _____

Modified cloze worksheet date	Percent correct

Notes:

Improving Skills Using Word-Sentence-Word Format

Objective: This tactic is designed to improve spelling ability.

Materials: Daily folder, four copies of the weekly spelling words worksheet (10–15 words), cassette player with headphones, cassette tapes, pencil, and Data Recording Sheet.

 Requires approximately **20 minutes** each day (one to two days per week).

Preparation: Make copies of tactic reproducibles and gather remaining tactic materials. Create a spelling word worksheet by writing the list of weekly spelling words in the left column of a piece of paper. Make four copies of the spelling word worksheet. Record each week's spelling words on audio cassette tapes (one cassette per student), using a word–sentence–word format: If the spelling word is "market," present the word "market," then a short pause, followed by a sentence, "The corn looked fresh at the *market*." Then provide a short pause, followed by the word "market" again. Give a three-second pause, and present the next word. Continue the process until all the words from the spelling word worksheet are recorded.

Coach Card

- ❏ Get materials (pencil, spelling word worksheet, cassette player, headphones, and cassette tape). Go to an assigned work area. Find the day's spelling word worksheet.

- ❏ Write names, grade, and date on the worksheet.

- ❏ **Student**: Put on the headphones with the cassette tape containing the week's recorded spelling word list.

- ❏ **Student**: Listen to the dictated spelling words while simultaneously looking at each word listed on the worksheet.

- ❏ **Student**: After listening to the tape, fold back the worksheet over the left column of spelling words to ensure that you cannot see the words.

- ❏ **Student**: Rewind and listen to the tape again, pausing the tape after each word and writing the word on the worksheet.

- ❏ **Student**: Score your paper by unfolding the worksheet and comparing the words you have written.

- ❏ **Student**: Count the number of words you spelled correctly. Correct your mistakes.

- ❏ **Student**: Write the number incorrect at the top of the page.

- ❏ **Coach**: Record results on the Data Recording Sheet.

Improving Skills Using Word–Sentence–Word Format: Data Recording Sheet

Student: _____   Grade: _____

Teacher: _____   Date begun:_____

                                                    Date ended:_____

Date	Number of spelling words	Number of words spelled correctly	Percent of words spelled correctly

Improving Skills Using Making Words

Objective: This tactic is designed to increase spelling ability.

Materials: Daily folder, weekly vocabulary word (choose a large word with many letters that can be used to form shorter words), making words worksheet (teacher-created; see Sample Worksheet), a list of shorter words containing the letters from the larger word, letter tiles (may be created from Letter Tiles sheet), timer, paper, pencil, and Data Recording Sheet.

 Requires approximately **15 minutes** each day (one to two times per week).

Preparation: Make copies of tactic reproducibles and gather remaining tactic materials. Select the final "big" word from a list of vocabulary words. Make a list of shorter words that can be made from the letters of the big word. From this list of words, select 12 to 15 words that emphasize an orthographic pattern you wish to teach or reinforce; include big and little words for differing ability levels of students, and words that can be made using the same letters in different positions (e.g., *words*, *sword*). Order the words according to the patterns and skills that will be emphasized; record this order of words. Create and then copy a making words worksheet, with large letters making up the big vocabulary word (scramble letters); also provide spaces for students to write two-, three-, and five-letter words made up from the letters in the big vocabulary word.

Coach Card

- ☐ Get materials. Go to an assigned work area. Find the day's making words worksheet containing the big vocabulary word.

- ☐ Write names, grade, and date on the worksheet.

- ☐ **Model**: Choose letter tiles that make up the big vocabulary word and scramble them on the table in front of the student.

- ☐ **Model**: Look at the scrambled letters that make up the big vocabulary word.

- ☐ **Model**: Using the letters, form two-letter words and write them on the lines provided.

- ☐ **Model**: Using the letters from the big vocabulary word, form three-letter words and write them on the lines provided.

- ☐ **Model**: Using the letters from the big vocabulary word, form five-letter words and write them on the lines provided..

- ☐ **Model**: Unscramble the big vocabulary word and write it on the last line provided.

- ☐ **Assessment**: Set the timer for three minutes. Instruct student to create as many words as possible, using the tiles, without assistance during the three-minute period. When timer buzzes, ask the student to stop.

- ☐ **Student**: Score your paper with help from the teacher or coach and correct your mistakes. Count the number of words you spelled correctly, writing the number correct at the top of the page.

- ☐ **Coach**: Record the results on the Data Recording Sheet.

Improving Skills Using Making Words: Letter Tiles

a	b	c	d
e	f	g	h
i	j	k	l
m	n	o	p
q	r	s	t
u	v	w	x
y	z		

Improving Skills Using Making Words:
Sample Worksheet

Student: _____ Grade: _____

Teacher: _____ Date: _____

$$\boxed{\textbf{testraiges}}$$

Two-letter words:

_____

_____

_____

_____

_____

Three-letter words:

_____

_____

_____

_____

_____

Five-letter words:

_____

_____

_____

_____

_____

_____

Big vocabulary word unscrambled:

_____

Improving Skills Using Making Words:
Data Recording Sheet

Student: _____ Grade: _____

Teacher: _____ Date begun:_____

Date ended:_____

Date	Number of words found	Number of words spelled correctly	Percent of words spelled correctly

Notes:

Improving Skills Using Word Walls

Objective: This tactic is designed to improve students' spelling skills.

Materials: Daily folder, bulletin board, weekly spelling word list, index cards, marker, timer, paper, pencil, and Data Recording Sheet.

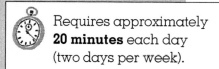
Requires approximately **20 minutes** each day (two days per week).

Preparation: Make copies of tactic reproducibles and gather remaining tactic materials. Choose a weekly spelling word list based on students' spelling ability level. Write the words on index cards and decorate the bulletin board with the index cards.

Coach Card

- ☐ Tell students, "You are going to review spelling words today."

- ☐ Tell students, "Get out a sheet of paper and write your name and date at the top."

- ☐ Call out a spelling word from the bulletin board.

- ☐ Instruct students to say the word.

- ☐ Chant the spelling of the word.

- ☐ Instruct students to chant the spelling of the word.

- ☐ Cover the word.

- ☐ Instruct students to write the word.

- ☐ Check spelling together.

- ☐ Continue introducing new words until the spelling word list is complete.

- ☐ **Assessment:** Set the timer for three minutes. Assess how well the student can spell the words that were practiced. Say each word, and have the student spell the word aloud in five seconds or less. Record the score on the Data Recording Sheet. Next, dictate each word aloud and have the student write each word on a sheet of paper. When the timer buzzes, ask the student to stop. Enter the scores on the Data Recording Sheet.

- ☐ **Coach:** Record individual results on each student's Data Recording Sheet.

Improving Skills Using Word Walls:
Data Recording Sheet

Student: _____ Grade: _____

Teacher: _____ Date begun:_____

Date ended:_____

Date	Number of words introduced	Number of words spelled correctly	Percent of words spelled correctly

Notes:

Improving Skills Using Add a Word

Objective: This tactic is designed to increase spelling performance.

Materials: Daily folder, problem words list, lined paper, pencil, timer, and Data Recording Sheet.

Preparation: Make copies of tactic reproducibles and gather remaining tactic materials. With help from the student, generate a list of "problem words." (Problem words should be continuously added to the problem words list.). Establish a set amount of time each day that will be devoted to practicing the spelling of the problem words.

Note: Should the student spell a problem word correctly for three consecutive days, the word is moved to the learned word file or list, which is maintained by the teacher. The word that is removed from the problem word list should be placed back on the problem word list after five to nine sessions; if the word is spelled correctly, it should be permanently removed from the problem word list.

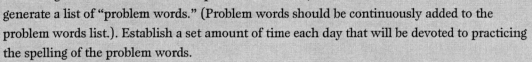

Requires approximately **15 minutes** each day (one to two days per week).

Coach Card

- ❑ Get materials. Go to an assigned work area. Find the day's problem word list.
- ❑ Write name and date on a piece of lined paper.
- ❑ **Coach**: Present the first word on the problem word list to the student by allowing the student to see the word.
- ❑ **Student**: Copy the word onto your paper.
- ❑ **Student**: Cover the word with a piece of paper.
- ❑ **Coach**: Say the word aloud.
- ❑ **Student**: Write the word from memory on your paper. If you are unable to write the word, say "I don't know that word."
- ❑ **Coach**: If the student does not know the word, have the student look at the word and spell it while looking at it. Next, have the student try to spell the word from memory.
- ❑ **Coach**: Praise the student if he/she knows the word, then proceed to the next word on list. Have the student score his/her paper with your assistance.
- ❑ **Assessment**: Set the timer for three minutes. Have the student use paper and pencil to spell as many words as possible within the three-minute period without assistance. The teacher will dictate the problem words. When the timer buzzes, ask the student to stop.
- ❑ **Coach**: Record results on the Data Recording Sheet.

Improving Skills Using Add a Word:
Data Recording Sheet

Student: _____   Grade: _____

Teacher: _____   Date: _____

Scoring instructions: Place a (+) in the correctly spelled column if the student writes the word correctly. Place a (/) in the incorrectly spelled column if the student spells the word incorrectly.

Problem spelling word	Correctly spelled	Incorrectly spelled

Notes:

Improving Skills Using the Write-Say Method

Objective: This tactic is designed to improve students' spelling skills.

Materials: Daily folder, weekly 10-item spelling word list, timer, lined paper, pencil, and Data Recording Sheet.

Preparation: Make copies of tactic reproducibles and gather remaining tactic materials. Each week, select 10 grade-appropriate spelling words to be learned and make a copy of the list for the student's daily folder.

> Requires approximately **10 minutes**.

Coach Card

- ❑ Get material. Go to an assigned work area. Write name and date on a sheet of lined paper.

- ❑ **Coach**: Find the weekly spelling word list.

- ❑ **Coach**: Say the first word aloud to the student, allowing time for the student to write the word.

- ❑ **Coach**: Check the spelling of the word written. (1) If the word is spelled correctly, go to the second word. (2) If the word is spelled incorrectly, show the student the correct spelling and instruct him/her to copy the correct spelling.

- ❑ **Coach**: Present the next word on the weekly spelling list by saying it aloud.

- ❑ **Coach**: Repeat the process until all words have been presented, spelled, and corrected.

- ❑ **Assessment**: Set the timer for three minutes. Call out spelling words from the list. Have the student spell as many words as possible without assistance within the three-minute period. When the timer buzzes, ask the student to stop.

- ❑ **Coach**: Record results on the Data Recording Sheet.

Improving Skills Using the Write–Say Method:
Data Recording Sheet

Student: _____   Grade: _____

Teacher: _____   Date begun:_____

                                                Date ended:_____

Date	Number of words introduced	Number of words spelled correctly	Percent of words spelled correctly	Percent of words spelled correctly

Notes:

Written Language Tactics

*My aim is to put down on paper what I see and
what I feel in the best and simplest way.*

—Ernest Hemingway (1899–1961)

Writing is an important component of the educational process. By the end of the primary grades, average-achieving students often have reached a level of fluency in the mechanics of writing that provides freedom in getting thoughts on paper (Graham & Harris, 1994). However, students who experience writing difficulty typically find the act of writing to be both difficult and unrewarding. A lack of motivation to write can lock students into a downward spiral in which they avoid most writing tasks and fail to develop critical writing skills. A lack of opportunities to practice writing skills can also be detrimental.

Students who find writing difficult vary in several ways from proficient writers. First, proficient writers use strategies to manage the tasks of planning, composing, and revising when writing. In contrast, students who have writing difficulties decrease the role of planning, revising, and other strategies. Second, proficient writers generate more ideas than they need, eliminating the less significant ideas as they write. Quite the reverse is characteristic of students with writing difficulties. They produce very little—their papers are very short and contain little detail or elaboration, and they are very hesitant to eliminate ideas. Third, unlike proficient writers, students with writing difficulties have trouble with the mechanics of writing such as spelling, capitalization, punctuation, and handwriting. They are less knowledgeable about writing and the writing process, and they emphasize form over substance.

Research suggests that developing writing proficiency depends on knowledge, skill, motivation, and self-regulation (Teale & Yokota, 2000). Writing can be taught. Both formal and informal teaching methods are critical to learning to write, especially for those with writing difficulties. Creative strategies need to be used to motivate students who dislike writing activities.

The written language tactics found in this chapter are designed to generate proficient writers through the use of explicit teaching and practice techniques. The tactics found at the beginning of this chapter focus on letter formation. Students must first learn to correctly form letters in order to form words and, eventually, paragraphs. Tactics entitled "Making Inferences/Comprehension 1" and "Providing Details/Comprehension 2" instruct the student to look at photographs of individuals and/or objects while making inferences and providing details in written form. The final tactics focus on brainstorming and using organization techniques to plan and eventually write a meaningful paragraph or multiple paragraphs. In the tactic titled "COPS Strategy," students are encouraged to check their own work through the use of a self-grading checklist, allowing them to be active participants in the learning process. Each tactic provides a Data Recording Sheet that is used to score written products.

Improving Letter Formation and Recognition Skills (Phases 1–3)

Objective: This tactic is designed to improve handwriting skills, letter formation, and letter recognition skills.

Materials: Daily folder, paper, pencil, index cards (pink and yellow), black marker, orange yarn, candy (reinforcer), daily practice worksheets (teacher-created), timer, and Data Recording Sheet.

 Each phase requires approximately **20 minutes** each day (one to two days per week).

Preparation: Make copies of tactic reproducibles and gather remaining tactic materials. Using the pink index cards and the black marker, print one letter of the student's name on one index card. For example, if the student's name is Meghan Doe, one index card would have an "M," another index card would have an "e," and so on. Continue this until each letter of the student's name is written in black marker on a pink index card. (The student's first and second initial should be written in uppercase, whereas the remainder of the letters should be written in lowercase.) Glue pieces of orange yarn arranged in the shape of each letter to each yellow index card. Gather or develop worksheets containing practice exercises for writing each letter in the student's name.

Note: This tactic involves three phases and has three Coach Cards.

M	e	g	h	a	n		D	o	e

Coach Card (Phase 1)

- ❏ Get materials (pencil, practice worksheet, and timer). Go to an assigned work area. Write name and date on paper.
- ❏ **Coach**: Show each pink card to the student.
- ❏ **Student**: Identify each letter shown to you.
- ❏ **Coach**: Instruct the student to write each of the letters on the sheet of paper (without looking back at the cards).
- ❏ **Student**: Write each letter shown on the index cards on your sheet of paper.
- ❏ **Assessment**: Set the timer for three minutes. Present the letters one at a time and have the student verbally identify, then write, as many letters as possible in the three-minute period without assistance. When the timer buzzes, stop.
- ❏ **Coach**: Record results on the Data Recording Sheet.

Improving Letter Formation and Recognition: Coach Card (Phase 2)

- ❏ Get materials (pencil, practice worksheet, and timer). Go to an assigned work area. Write name and date on paper.

- ❏ **Coach**: Present each yellow card with letters formed in orange yarn to the student.

- ❏ **Student**: Verbally identify each letter presented.

- ❏ **Coach**: If the student responds correctly (all letters correct), present him/her with the chosen reinforcer.

- ❏ **Coach**: If the student responds incorrectly, instruct the student to outline the shape of the letter on the index card using his/her fingertip.

- ❏ **Assessment**: Set the timer for three minutes. Present letters one at a time, and have the student verbally identify, then write, as many letters as possible without assistance within the three-minute period. When the timer buzzes, stop.

- ❏ **Coach**: Record results on the Data Recording Sheet.

Improving Letter Formation and Recognition: Coach Card (Phase 3)

- ❏ Get materials (pencil, practice worksheet, and timer). Go to an assigned work area. Write name and date on paper.

- ❏ **Coach**: Instruct the student to print his/her name on a sheet of paper without using the model letters.

- ❏ **Student**: Write your name on the sheet of paper.

- ❏ **Coach**: Provide verbal prompts to encourage the student to self-evaluate.

- ❏ **Assessment**: Set the timer for three minutes. Present the letters one at a time, and have the student verbally identify, then write, as many letters as possible without assistance within the three-minute period. When the timer buzzes, stop.

- ❏ **Coach**: Record results on the Data Recording Sheet.

Improving Letter Formation and Recognition Skills (Phases 1–3): Data Recording Sheet

Student: _____ Grade: _____

Teacher: _____ Date: _____

Scoring instructions: Write one letter of the student's name on each line of the Letters column. Place a plus (+) in the columns if the student recognizes (identifies) or forms (writes) the letter correctly. Place a slash (/) in the columns if the student incorrectly identifies or writes letter.

Letters	Letter recognition	Letter formation	Phase 1, 2, or 3?
M	+	+	
e	/	/	
g	+	+	
h	+	+	
a	+	+	
n	+	+	
D	+	+	
o	+	+	
e	/	/	

Notes:

Practicing Letter Formation

Objective: This tactic is designed to improve students' handwriting ability and improve copying skills.

Materials: Daily folder, paper, pencil, chalk or marker, timer, and Data Recording Sheet.

Preparation: Make copies of tactic reproducibles and gather remaining tactic materials. Collect daily practice writings in the student's daily folder.

Note: This tactic can be used with individual students or the classroom as a whole.

 Requires approximately **20 minutes** each day (one to two days per week).

Coach Card

- ❑ **Coach**: Instruct students to take out a piece of paper and a pencil.

- ❑ Select a group of letters to be practiced.

- ❑ Tell the students that they will be practicing selected letters by copying and writing letters from the board.

- ❑ Make sure students place their pencils flat on their desks.

- ❑ Direct students' attention to the board.

- ❑ Introduce each letter by writing the letter on the board, where a representation of lined paper has been drawn beforehand.

- ❑ **Coach**: As you write the letter, explain what you are doing. For example, "To make a 't,' I start at the top of the line and draw a straight line down to the bottom line, then I lift my pencil off the paper and move it to the middle of the straight line. I then cross the line with a short line like this."

- ❑ Have the students repeat the verbalized identification and written stroke sequence.

- ❑ Have the students copy and verbalize each letter presented several times until all of the selected letters have been introduced.

- ❑ **Assessment**: Set the timer for three minutes. Call out the selected letters randomly and have students write as many letters as they can without assistance during the three-minute period. When the timer buzzes, ask the students to stop writing.

- ❑ **Coach**: Record results on individual Data Recording Sheets.

Practicing Letter Formation: Data Recording Sheet

Student: _____   Grade: _____

Teacher: _____   Date: _____

Letters	Letter formed correctly	Letter formed incorrectly
A a		
B b		
C c		
D d		
E e		
F f		
G g		
H h		
I i		
J j		
K k		
L l		
M m		
N n		
O o		
P p		
Q q		
R r		
S s		
T t		
U u		
V v		
W w		
X x		
Y y		
Z z		

Notes:

Improving Letter Formation While Teaching Initial Consonants

Objective: This tactic is designed to build accuracy with letter formation while simultaneously teaching initial letter-sound recognition.

 Requires approximately **15 minutes** each day (two to three days per week).

Materials: Daily folder, Picture/Letter Cards for Consonants, Random Consonant Letters Worksheet, See-to-Write Worksheet, timer, and Data Recording Sheet.

Preparation: Make copies of tactic reproducibles and gather remaining tactic materials. Cut out a set of the Picture/Letter Cards for Consonants or construct a set of your own, ensuring that the picture appears on one side and the initial consonant letter sound appears on the other. Construct a worksheet with the same consonant letters arranged for writing letter practice. Construct a worksheet containing all the uppercase/lowercase consonant letters, listed randomly, for curriculum-based assessment.

Coach Card

❑ Get materials. Go to an assigned work area.

❑ Present each picture card to the student and have the student name the picture, verbally prompting the student when necessary.

❑ Instruct the student to name the beginning letter of the picture card. Have the student turn the picture card over and say the letter while tracing the letter with his/her finger. Do this for each practice letter.

❑ Have the student practice writing letters on the See-to-Write Worksheet, saying each letter as it's written.

❑ **Assessment**: After practice, assess the student by using the Random Consonant Letters Worksheet. Set the timer for one minute. Instruct the student to say each letter on the worksheet. When the timer buzzes, ask the student to stop.

❑ **Coach**: Count the number of correct/incorrect letters identified and record the results on the Data Recording Sheet.

Improving Letter Formation While Teaching Initial Consonants: Picture/Letter Cards for Consonants

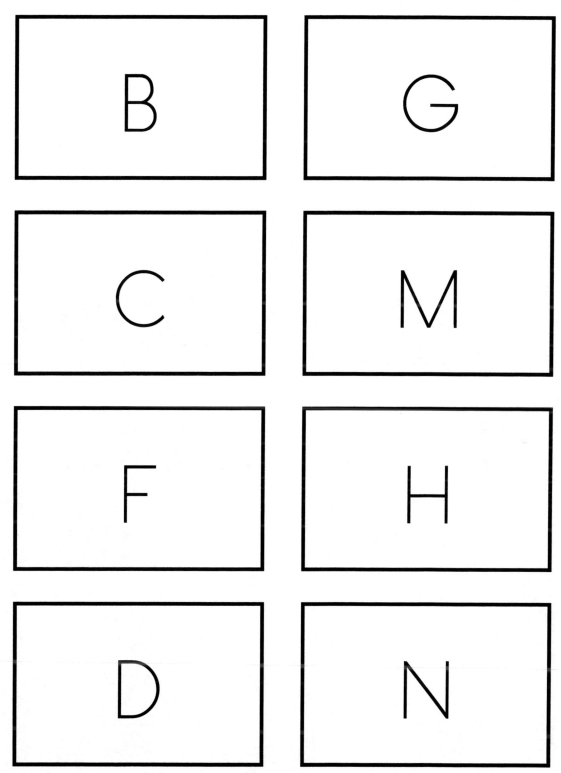

Chapter 3 • *Tactics for Boosting Academic Achievement*   Improving Letter Formation While Teaching Initial Consonants

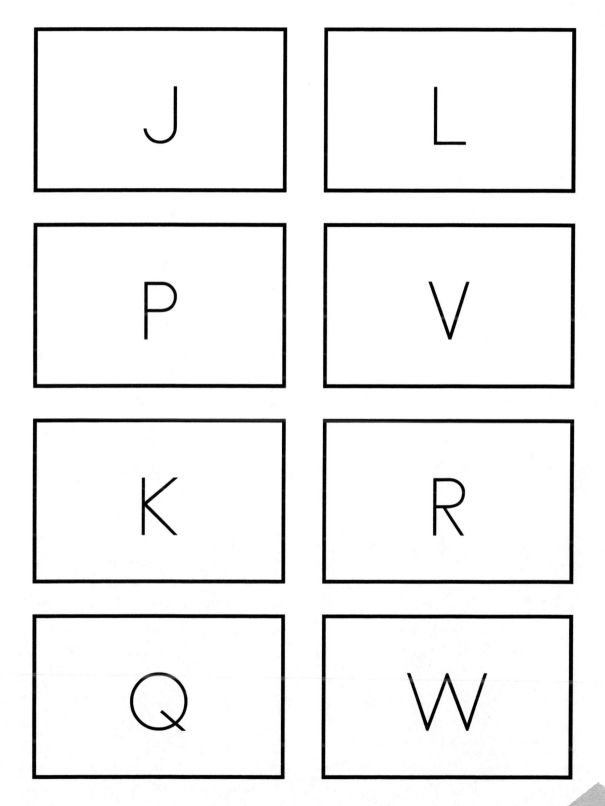

159

Improving Letter Formation While Teaching Initial Consonants   *Tactics for Boosting Academic Achievement* • Chapter 3

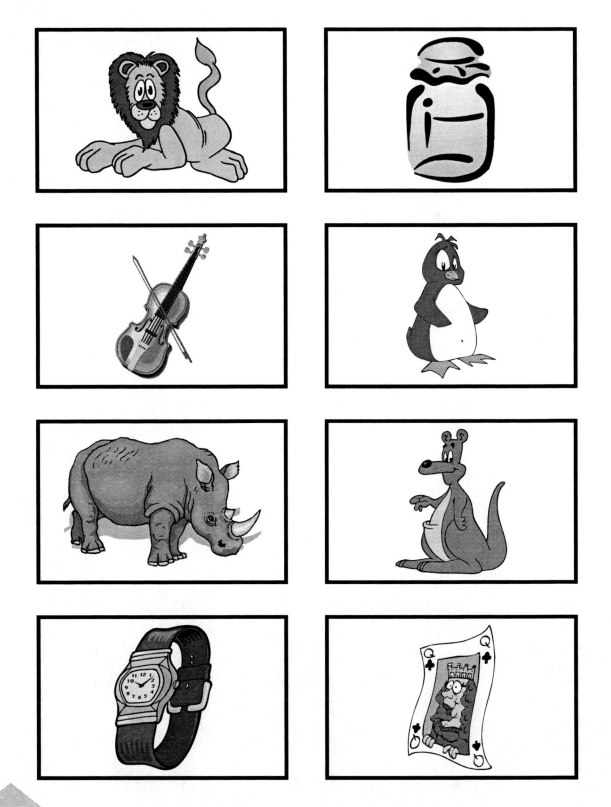

Chapter 3 • *Tactics for Boosting Academic Achievement*   Improving Letter Formation While Teaching Initial Consonants

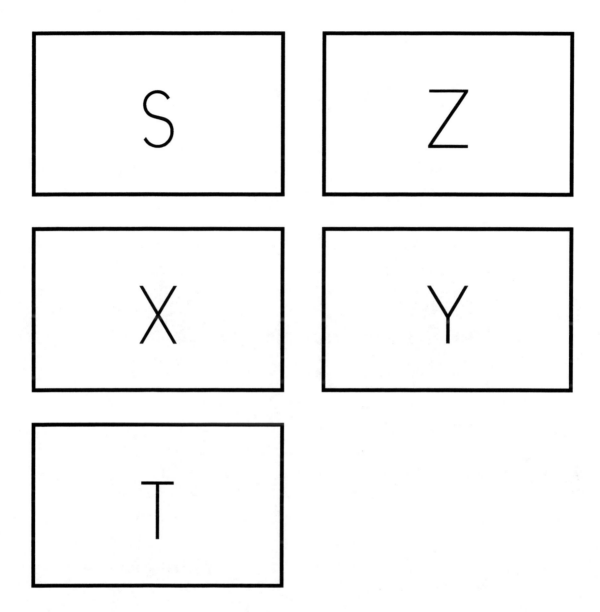

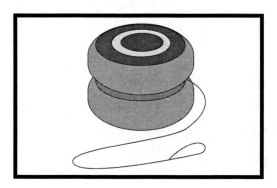

Chapter 3 • *Tactics for Boosting Academic Achievement*   Improving Letter Formation While Teaching Initial Consonants

Improving Letter Formation While Teaching Initial Consonants: Random Consonant Letters Worksheet

G	p	c
b	L	m
f	K	W
s	q	k
V	J	n
J	g	r
D	h	Z
T	x	G

Improving Letter Formation While Teaching
Initial Consonants: See-to-Write Worksheet

Student: _____   Grade: _____

Teacher: _____   Date: _____

B _____   b _____

C _____   c _____

D _____   d _____

F _____   f _____

G _____   g _____

H _____   h _____

J _____   j _____

K _____   k _____

L _____   l _____

M _____   m _____

N _____   n _____

P _____   p _____

Q _____   q _____

R _____   r _____

S _____   s _____

T _____   t _____

V _____   v _____

W _____   w _____

X _____   x _____

Z _____   z _____

Improving Letter Formation While Teaching
Initial Consonants: Data Recording Sheet

Student: _____ Grade: _____

Teacher: _____ Date: _____

Date	Number of letters identified correctly	Number of letters identified incorrectly	Letters needing work

Notes:

Writing the One-Paragraph Outline

Objective: This tactic is designed to improve the writing process.

Materials: Daily folder, Idea Light Bulb Worksheet, One-Paragraph Outline Worksheet (see Sample One-Paragraph Outline Worksheet), timer, colored pencils, and Data Recording Sheet.

 Requires approximately **30–45 minutes** each day (one to two days per week).

Preparation: Make copies of tactic reproducibles and gather remaining tactic materials. Provide a topic to beginners. Students with more advanced writing skills should be given the opportunity to choose a topic to write about prior to beginning this tactic. Different topics should be used each time the tactic is used.

Note: This tactic is suitable for individuals or for groups of students.

Coach Card

- ❑ Get materials. Go to an assigned work area.

- ❑ Using the Idea Light Bulb Worksheet, brainstorm and write ideas about the topic the teacher has provided or the topic you have chosen.

- ❑ Choose four or five of the ideas from your completed Worksheet to use in writing a paragraph.

- ❑ Using colored pencils and the color codes presented on the One-Paragraph Outline Worksheet, color code the "ideas" chosen on the Idea Light Bulb Worksheet to be used in writing the paragraph.

- ❑ Complete a first draft of the One-Paragraph Outline Worksheet.

- ❑ Present the first draft of your One-Paragraph Outline Worksheet to the teacher or coach for feedback.

- ❑ **Coach**: Read over the first draft of the worksheet and make comments.

- ❑ **Coach**: Ask the student to correct/rewrite his/her first draft worksheet. Time for two minutes.

- ❑ **Student Self-Assessment**: Using the Data Recording Sheet, assess your rewritten worksheet.

- ❑ **Coach**: Using the Data Recording Sheet, score the student's rewritten worksheet.

Writing the One-Paragraph Outline:
Idea Light Bulb Worksheet

Student: _____   Grade: _____

Teacher: _____   Date: _____

Topic: _____

Writing the One-Paragraph Outline: Sample Worksheet

Student: <u>Amanda</u>   Grade: <u>4</u>

Teacher: <u>Mr. Henry</u>   Date: <u>April 8</u>

   I. Topic: <u>My cat.</u>

  II. Topic sentence (green): <u>My cat, Kate, is cute and lives in my room.</u>

 III. Supporting detail (yellow): <u>She has yellow fur and a long yellow tail.</u>

 IV. Supporting detail (yellow): <u>Her favorite toy is a ball.</u>

  V. Supporting detail (yellow): <u>Kate sleeps on a pillow in my room.</u>

 VI. Concluding sentence (red): <u>I am so glad she is my cat.</u>

Outline feedback (coach comments):

From reading your paragraph, I feel that your topic was <u>about your pet</u>.

I liked the part when <u>you told me where she sleeps</u>. I think there could be

improvements <u>if you added more details about the things your cat does</u>. I see

you have included:

1.   A topic sentence: Yes

2.   Three supporting details: Yes

3.   A concluding sentence: Yes

Writing the One-Paragraph Outline:
Outline Feedback

Student: _____   Grade: _____

Teacher: _____   Date: _____

   I. Topic:_____

       _____

  II. Topic sentence (green): _____

       _____

 III. Supporting detail (yellow): _____

       _____

 IV. Supporting detail (yellow): _____

       _____

  V. Supporting detail (yellow): _____

       _____

 VI. Concluding sentence (red):_____

       _____

Outline feedback (coach comments):

_____

_____

_____

_____

_____

_____

_____

_____

_____

Writing the One-Paragraph Outline: Data Recording Sheet

Student: _____ Grade: _____

Teacher: _____ Date: _____

Directions: Circle appropriate number.

Ideas and content

5 Clearly conveys one main idea, theme, or topic with relevant supporting details. Written from experience showing insight. Holds reader's attention.

3 Conveys one main idea, theme, or topic with little or no supporting details. Little or no insight from writer. Does not hold reader's attention.

1 Unrecognizable main idea, theme, or topic.

0 No attempt.

Organization

5 Introduction grabs reader. Satisfying conclusion. Well sequenced details. Smooth transitions. Easy to read.

3 Identifiable introduction. Identifiable conclusion. Lacks smoothly sequenced details. Attempts to use transitions. Difficult to follow at times.

0 Unrecognizable introduction. Unrecognizable conclusion. Confusing details.

0 No attempt.

Voice

5 Written from the heart. Written with a reader in mind. Reader can feel the person behind the words. Expressive.

3 Written sincerely. Written to please the reader. Pleasant, but not engaging. Inconsistent style.

0 Functionally correct. Completely lifeless.

0 No attempt.

Word choice

5   Vocabulary is strong, but not overdone. Words sound natural. Verbs are powerful. Nouns are specific. Strong visual imagery.

3   Vocabulary correct, but common. Uses cliches and slang. Clear but imprecise. "Generic."

0   Incorrect vocabulary. Repetitive. Weak verbs (is, are, was, were).

0   No attempt.

Sentence fluency

5   Clearly written. Easy to read aloud. Varies in length and structure. Rhythmic and natural.

3   Clearly written. Somewhat awkward to read aloud. Little variation in sentence structure. Efficient, but not rhythmic.

1   Incomplete sentences. Impossible to read aloud. Makes no sense.

0   No attempt.

Conventions

5   Uses correct grammar. Uses needed punctuation. Uses correct spelling. Uses correct paragraphing. Writing is easy to read and ready for publication.

3   Grammar errors do not distort meaning. Ending punctuation is correct. Spelling is correct or phonetic. Paragraphing inconsistent. Writing reads less smoothly and needs moderate editing.

1   Numerous errors in grammar, punctuation, and spelling. Writing nearly impossible to read for meaning.

0   No attempt.

Using Dialogue Journals

Objective: This tactic is designed to improve students' writing and communication skills through the utilization of a dialogue journal.

Materials: dialogue journal, pencil, timer, daily folder, and Data Recording Sheet.

Preparation: Make copies of tactic reproducibles and gather remaining tactic materials. Develop a list of various "story starters" (see Sample Story Starters) for use as motivational tools for writing.

 Requires approximately **15 minutes** each day (one to two days per week).

Coach Card

- ❑ Get materials. Go to an assigned work area.
- ❑ Find the day's writing page in your dialogue journal.
- ❑ Write your name and date on the page.
- ❑ Read the teacher's "story starter" journal entry.
- ❑ Respond to the teacher by writing a short paragraph.
- ❑ Place the completed dialogue journal in a designated spot.
- ❑ **Coach**: Read and respond to the student writings.
- ❑ **Assessment**: Set the timer for three minutes. Instruct the student to write in the dialogue journal as many words as he/she can during the three-minute period. When the timer buzzes, ask the student to stop.
- ❑ **Coach**: Read and respond to student writings. Record the number of words written and number of words spelled incorrectly on the Data Recording Sheet. Place the dialogue journal in a designated spot for easy student access.

Using Dialogue Journals:
Sample Story Starters

The phone rang and …

I heard a sound outside my window …

The wind blew so hard …

One day during class …

When I went home …

If I had a million dollars …

When I grow up I want to be …

My favorite birthday gift is …

While walking through the woods one day …

I found a box outside my door …

The airplane began to sputter …

When I turned on the television I saw …

When I looked in the mirror I saw …

A tornado was heading straight for my house …

My spaghetti began to talk …

The ground began moving …

I saw a Leprechaun in my cereal …

While I was playing on the sidewalk, a strange car drove up beside me …

When I arrived home from school, no one was home …

Over the weekend, I …

During summer break …

Using Dialogue Journals:
Data Recording Sheet

Student: _____   Grade: _____

Teacher: _____   Date: _____

Date	Number of words written	Number of words spelled correctly	Percent of words spelled correctly

Notes:

Using the COPS Strategy

Objective: This tactic is designed to help students identify four error types when writing paragraphs.

Materials: Daily folder, paper, pencil, and Data Recording Sheet.

 Requires approximately **15 minutes** each day (one to two times per week).

Preparation: Make copies of tactic reproducibles and gather remaining tactic materials. Teachers should provide topics to beginners. Students with more advanced writing skills should be instructed to choose their own topic. A different topic should be used each time the tactic is used. Instruct the student to write a paragraph/story on a chosen topic, then complete the steps on the Coach Card.

Coach Card

- ❏ Get materials. Go to an assigned work area. Write a paragraph/story on the chosen topic.
- ❏ **Model: C** – CAPITALIZATION
  - ○ Is the first word of each sentence capitalized?
  - ○ Are proper nouns capitalized?
- ❏ **Model: O** – OVERALL appearance of work
  - ○ Check for neatness.
  - ○ Are words written legibly?
  - ○ Check margins.
  - ○ Are paragraphs indented properly?
  - ○ Did you use complete sentences?
- ❏ **Model: P** – PUNCTUATION
  - ○ Check comma usage.
  - ○ Check ending punctuation.
- ❏ **Model: S** – SPELLING
  - ○ Are words spelled correctly?
- ❏ Place your completed paragraph/story and Coach Card in your daily folder
- ❏ **Assessment**: Using Data Recording Sheet, evaluate the student's paragraph/story and record the results.

Using the COPS Strategy:
Checklist

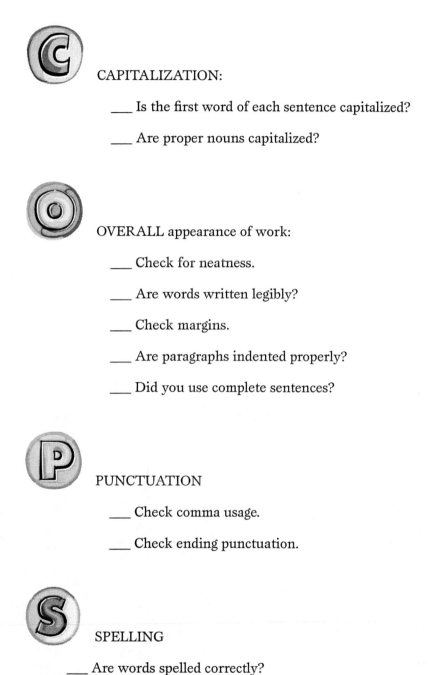

CAPITALIZATION:

___ Is the first word of each sentence capitalized?

___ Are proper nouns capitalized?

OVERALL appearance of work:

___ Check for neatness.

___ Are words written legibly?

___ Check margins.

___ Are paragraphs indented properly?

___ Did you use complete sentences?

PUNCTUATION

___ Check comma usage.

___ Check ending punctuation.

SPELLING

___ Are words spelled correctly?

Using the COPS Strategy: Data Recording Sheet

Student: _____   Grade: _____

Teacher: _____   Date: _____

COPS components	COPS subcomponents	Points possible	Points earned
CAPITALIZATION	First words of sentences capitalized	5	
	Proper nouns capitalized	5	
OVERALL appearance of work	Neat	5	
	Legibly written	4	
	Margins used correctly	3	
	Paragraphs properly indented	4	
	Complete sentences used	4	
PUNCTUATION	Commas used correctly	5	
	Correct ending punctuation used	5	
SPELLING	Correct spelling used	5	
	Total	45	

Notes:

Writing Multiple Paragraphs

Objective: This tactic is designed to improve the
writing process.

Materials: Daily folder, pencil, Idea Light Bulb Worksheet,
Five-Paragraph Outline Worksheet, timer, and Data
Recording Sheet.

 Requires approximately
30–45 minutes each
day (one to two times
per week).

Preparation: Make copies of tactic reproducibles and gather
remaining tactic materials. Provide a topic to beginners. Students with more advanced writing
skills should be instructed to choose their own topic. Different topics should be used each time
the tactic is used.

Note: This tactic is suitable for individuals and for groups of students.

Coach Card

- ❑ Get materials. Go to an assigned work area.

- ❑ Using the Idea Light Bulb Worksheet, brainstorm and write ideas about the topic the
  teacher has provided or the topic you have chosen.

- ❑ Choose four or five ideas from your completed worksheet to use in writing a story.

- ❑ Using the Five-Paragraph Outline Worksheet, arrange your chosen ideas to complete a
  first draft, and then present it to the teacher or coach for feedback.

- ❑ **Coach**: Read over the first draft of the worksheet and make comments.

- ❑ **Assessment**: Ask the student to correct/rewrite his/her first draft worksheet.

- ❑ **Student self-assessment**: Using the Data Recording Sheet, assess your
  rewritten worksheet.

- ❑ **Coach**: Using the Data Recording Sheet, score the student's rewritten worksheet.

Writing Multiple Paragraphs:
Idea Light Bulb Worksheet

Student: _____   Grade: _____

Teacher: _____   Date: _____

Topic: _____

Writing Multiple Paragraphs: Five-Paragraph Outline

Student: _____ Grade: _____

Teacher: _____ Date: _____

I. Introduction

    A. General _____

    B. Narrowed focus _____

    C. Specific _____

II. Topic 1

    A. _____

    B. _____

    C. _____

    D. Transition _____

III. Topic 2

    A. _____

    B. _____

    C. _____

    D. Transition _____

IV. Topic 3

    A. _____

    B. _____

    C. _____

    D. Transition _____

(continued on next page)

V. Conclusion

    A. Introduction topic _____

        _____

    B. Feelings _____

        _____

    C. Ending sentence _____

        _____

Writing Multiple Paragraphs:
Data Recording Sheet

Student: _____   Grade: _____

Teacher: _____   Date: _____

Directions: Circle appropriate number.

Ideas and content

6   Clearly conveys one main idea, theme, or topic with relevant supporting details. Written from experience showing insight. Holds reader's attention.

4   Conveys one main idea, theme, or topic with little or no supporting details. Little or no insight from writer. Does not hold reader's attention.

2   Unrecognizable main idea, theme, or topic.

0   No attempt.

Organization

6   Introduction grabs reader. Satisfying conclusion. Well sequenced details. Smooth transitions. Easy to read.

3   Identifiable introduction. Identifiable conclusion. Lacks smoothly sequenced details. Attempts to use transitions. Difficult to follow at times.

1   Unrecognizable introduction. Unrecognizable conclusion. Confusing details.

1   No attempt.

Voice

5   Written from the heart. Written with a reader in mind. Reader can feel the person behind the words. Expressive.

3   Written sincerely. Written to please the reader. Pleasant, but not engaging. Inconsistent style.

0   Functionally correct. Completely lifeless.

0   No attempt.

Word choice

5 Vocabulary is strong, but not overdone. Words sound natural. Verbs are powerful. Nouns are specific. Strong visual imagery.

3 Vocabulary correct, but common. Uses cliches and slang. Clear but imprecise. "Generic."

1 Incorrect vocabulary. Repetitive. Weak verbs (is, are, was, were).

0 No attempt.

Sentence fluency

5 Clearly written. Easy to read aloud. Varies in length and structure. Rhythmic and natural.

3 Clearly written. Somewhat awkward to read aloud. Little variation in sentence structure. Efficient, but not rhythmic.

1 Incomplete sentences. Impossible to read aloud. Makes no sense.

1 No attempt.

Conventions

5 Uses correct grammar. Uses needed punctuation. Uses correct spelling. Uses correct paragraphing. Writing is easy to read and ready for publication.

3 Grammar errors do not distort meaning. Ending punctuation is correct. Spelling is correct or phonetic. Paragraphing inconsistent. Writing reads less smoothly and needs moderate editing.

1 Numerous errors in grammar, punctuation, and spelling. Writing nearly impossible to read for meaning.

0 No attempt.

Mathematics Tactics

Not everything that counts can be counted and
not everything that can be counted counts.

—*Albert Einstein*

Helping students develop an understanding of basic mathematical concepts and procedures is a fundamental goal of schooling. All students need to acquire the knowledge and skills to figure out the math-related problems they will encounter in their adult lives. Mathematics is made up of two categories of skills: math calculation and math reasoning. Research findings in mathematics indicate that students can benefit from instructional strategies that include both explicit and implicit methods (Mercer, Jordan, & Miller, 1994). Research supports the use of explicit methods, such as description of procedures, modeling of skills (teacher uses "think-aloud" or describes the thinking process as math problems are solved), use of cues and prompts, direct questioning of students to ensure understanding, and practice to mastery. Research also supports the use of implicit methods to teach math. Examples of such methods are reflection on learning, linking information to prior knowledge, and discovery.

Poor math achievement may result from difficulties differentiating numbers and copying shapes (poor visual perception), recalling math facts (memory problems), writing numbers legibly or in small spaces (weak motor functions), and relating math terms to meaning (poor understanding of math-related vocabulary). Other weak areas may include abstract reasoning (solving word problems and making comparisons) and metacognition (including identifying, using, and monitoring the use of algorithms to solve math problems).

The math tactics included in this chapter were chosen to address the problems mentioned in the previous paragraph. Chapter 4 begins with tactics that focus on patterns and functions, seriation and classification of objects, and preoperational classification and sorting—all areas that must be understood during the beginning phases of mathematics instruction. Next in the chapter are various tactics designed to improve number recognition, followed by tactics that include sequencing and writing numbers and various tactics for teaching multiplication facts. The chapter ends with numerous tactics used to solve math word problems. The tactics addressing math word problems, like all other tactics in this chapter, are presented in an order that begins with the use of manipulatives and progresses to nonmanipulative techniques. These final tactics also introduce ways to organize the information presented in each word problem, thus resulting in a better understanding of what is being asked. Furthermore, the tactics are designed to teach students using the direct instruction approach; coaches may be used for most of the tactics.

Understanding Patterns and Functions

Objective: This tactic is designed to improve understanding of patterns.

Materials: Daily folder, container of dominoes, Domino Examination Worksheet, Sample Domino Patterns, paper, pencil, timer, and Data Recording Sheet.

Preparation: Make copies of tactic reproducibles and gather remaining tactic materials. Prior to tactic implementation, introduce the student to patterns using the Sample Domino Patterns reproducible. Review checklist steps with the student.

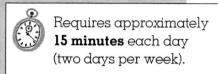

Requires approximately **15 minutes** each day (two days per week).

Coach Card

☐ Get materials. Go to an assigned work area. Get a sheet of paper and write your name and date on it.

☐ Take the dominoes from the container.

☐ Position two or more dominoes to form a pattern. See Sample Domino Patterns for examples.

☐ Write the pattern numbers on the Domino Examination Worksheet and answer the questions.

☐ **Assessment**: Set the timer for two minutes. Have the student arrange as many dominoes in patterns as possible without assistance during the two-minute period. When the timer buzzes, ask the student to stop.

☐ **Coach**: Record results on the Data Recording Sheet.

Understanding Patterns and Functions: Domino Examination Worksheet

Student: _____   Grade: _____

Teacher: _____   Date: _____

Instructions: Examine the dominoes, write the pattern numbers below, and answer the following questions.

1. Is the number of dots on one half greater than the number on the other half?

    _____

2. Are both halves of each domino the same?

    _____

3. Are they both even or odd numbers?

    _____

Understanding Patterns and Functions:
Sample Domino Patterns

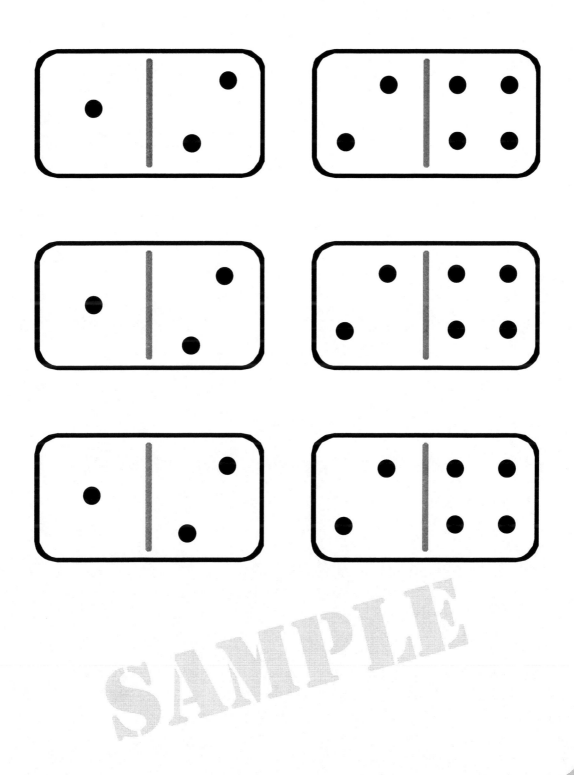

Understanding Patterns and Functions:
Data Recording Sheet

Student: _____   Grade: _____

Teacher: _____   Date begun:_____

                                               Date ended:_____

Date	Number of dominoes used in pattern	Number of dominoes correctly ordered	Percent of dominoes correctly ordered

Notes:

Creating Patterns

Objective: This tactic is designed to increase the student's ability to create patterns.

Materials: Daily folder, Pattern Worksheet, colored UNIFIX® cubes, timer, colored pencils or crayons, and Data Recording Sheet.

Preparation: Make copies of tactic reproducibles and gather remaining tactic materials. Use UNIFIX cubes (math manipulatives) to model patterns.

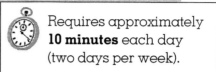

Requires approximately **10 minutes** each day (two days per week).

Coach Card

- ❑ Gather materials. Go to an assigned work area.

- ❑ **Model**: Find the Pattern Worksheet and cover all rows except the one being used.

- ❑ Place one colored UNIFIX cube on or above each square to make a pattern. Say each color aloud. Show the student how to continue the pattern, naming the color of each UNIFIX cube used. Repeat this procedure three times, completing one row of the Pattern Worksheet.

- ❑ Show the student how to make a pattern by coloring in the squares. Repeat this procedure two times.

- ❑ **Guided practice**: Instruct the student to cover all rows on the Pattern Worksheet except the one being used.

- ❑ Instruct the student to place one colored UNIFIX cube on or above each square to make a pattern. Ask the student to say each color aloud.

- ❑ Instruct the student to continue the pattern by placing the UNIFIX cubes on the corresponding squares. Repeat this procedure three times, completing one row of the Pattern Worksheet.

- ❑ Begin a pattern by coloring in the squares on a blank row of the Pattern Worksheet. Instruct the student to complete the pattern by filling in the rest of the squares. If the student does not respond within ten seconds, tell the student the next color and review the pattern with him/her. Repeat this procedure two times, completing two rows on the Pattern Worksheet.

- ❑ **Assessment**: Set the timer for two minutes. Cover all rows except the one being used. Begin a pattern on the Pattern Worksheet by coloring in the squares. Instruct the student to finish coloring in the squares to complete the pattern. Repeat this procedure with the student as many times as possible without assistance during the two-minute period. When the timer buzzes, stop.

- ❑ **Coach**: Record results on the Data Recording Sheet.

Creating Patterns: Pattern Worksheet

Student: _____   Grade: _____

Teacher: _____   Date: _____

Instructions: Complete the pattern by coloring in the squares.

Creating Patterns: Data Recording Sheet

Student: _____ Grade: _____

Teacher: _____ Date begun: _____

Date ended: _____

Date	Number of patterns completed correctly	Number of patterns completed incorrectly	Number of patterns attempted

Notes:

Arranging and Classifying Objects by Size

Objective: This tactic is designed to increase the student's ability to put objects in order by size (smallest to largest and/or largest to smallest).

Materials: Daily folder, Objects Sheets 1–5, scissors, pencil, timer, and Data Recording Sheet.

Preparation: Make copies of tactic reproducibles and gather remaining tactic materials. Cut out all objects from each Object Sheet.

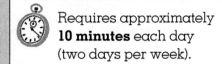

Requires approximately **10 minutes** each day (two days per week).

Coach Card

- ☐ Get materials. (Begin with three objects and add more as the student masters them.) Go to an assigned work area.

- ☐ **Model**: Place a set of objects, out of order, on the table.

- ☐ **Coach**: Model placing the objects in a row in order from smallest to largest, verbally describing what you are doing.

- ☐ Repeat the two steps above for at least five sets of objects, but put objects in order from largest to smallest.

- ☐ Guided practice: Place a set of objects, out of order, in front of the student.

- ☐ Instruct the student to put them in order from smallest to largest.

- ☐ **Coach**: Mix them up again and instruct the student to place them in order from largest to smallest. *Encourage the student to compare the sizes of the objects by placing them next to or on top of each other.* Repeat this procedure five times.

- ☐ **Assessment**: Place sets of objects in front of the student. Set the timer for two minutes. Instruct the student to place the objects in order from smallest to largest, then largest to smallest. When the timer rings, ask the student to stop.

- ☐ **Coach**: Record results on the Data Recording Sheet.

Arranging and Classifying Objects by Size:
Objects Sheet 1

Arranging and Classifying Objects by Size:
Objects Sheet 2

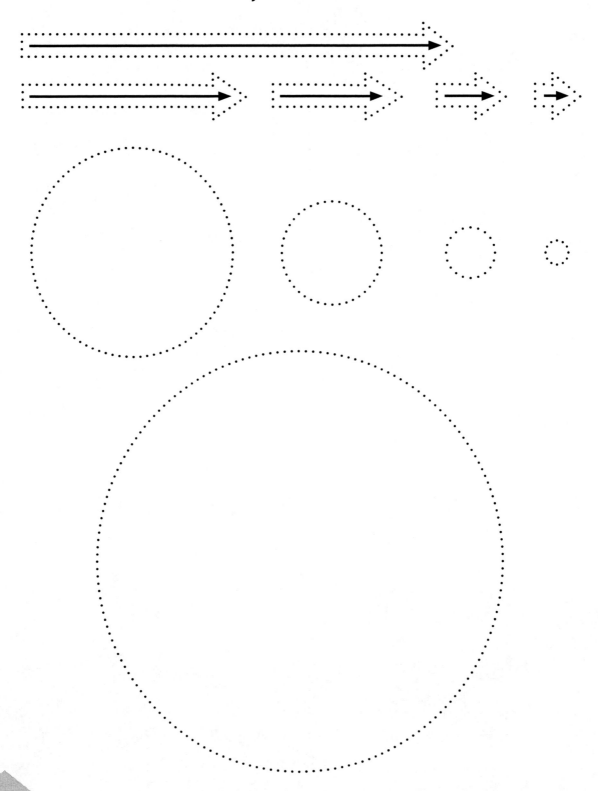

Arranging and Classifying Objects by Size:
Objects Sheet 3

Arranging and Classifying Objects by Size:
Objects Sheet 4

© Sopris West Educational Services. This page may be photocopied.

Arranging and Classifying Objects by Size:
Objects Sheet 5

Arranging and Classifying Objects by Size:
Data Recording Sheet

Student: _____ Grade: _____

Teacher: _____ Date begun:_____

Date ended:_____

Date	Number of sets attempted	Number of sets completed correctly	Number of sets completed incorrectly

Notes:

Developing Preoperational Classification and Sorting Skills

Objective: This tactic is designed to increase the student's ability to classify or sort one dimensionally.

Materials: Daily folder, Object Classification Worksheet, Object Classification Assessment, scissors, pencil, timer, and Data Recording Sheet.

Preparation: Make copies of tactic reproducibles and gather remaining tactic materials. Cut out all objects from the Object Classification Worksheet.

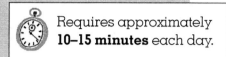

Requires approximately **10–15 minutes** each day.

Coach Card

- ❑ Get materials. Go to an assigned work area.
- ❑ Set the timer for 15 minutes.
- ❑ **Model**: Find the Worksheet cut outs. Choose three objects: two that are the same and one that is different or does not look like the others.
- ❑ Place the three objects in a row in front of the student. Show the student which square is different from the others and explain why.
- ❑ Repeat the last two steps for at least three different sets of objects.
- ❑ **Guided practice**: Instruct the student to point to the object that is different or does not look like the others in the set and explain why it is different.
- ❑ Using the timer, allow ten seconds of wait time and then tell the student the answer if necessary.
- ❑ Repeat the last two steps for five different sets of objects.
- ❑ **Assessment**: Give the student an Object Classification Assessment sheet. Cover all rows with a blank piece of paper, leaving one row for the student to see. Instruct the student to point to the object that is different or does not look like the others, doing the same for as many rows as possible during the two minutes. When the timer rings, stop.
- ❑ **Coach**: Record the results on the Data Recording Sheet.

© Sopris West Educational Services. This page may be photocopied. **201**

Developing Preoperational Classification and Sorting Skills · *Tactics for Boosting Academic Achievement* • Chapter 4

Developing Preoperational Classification and Sorting Skills: Object Classification Worksheet

Instructions: Cut out objects. Arrange in sets of three or more with one different object in each set.

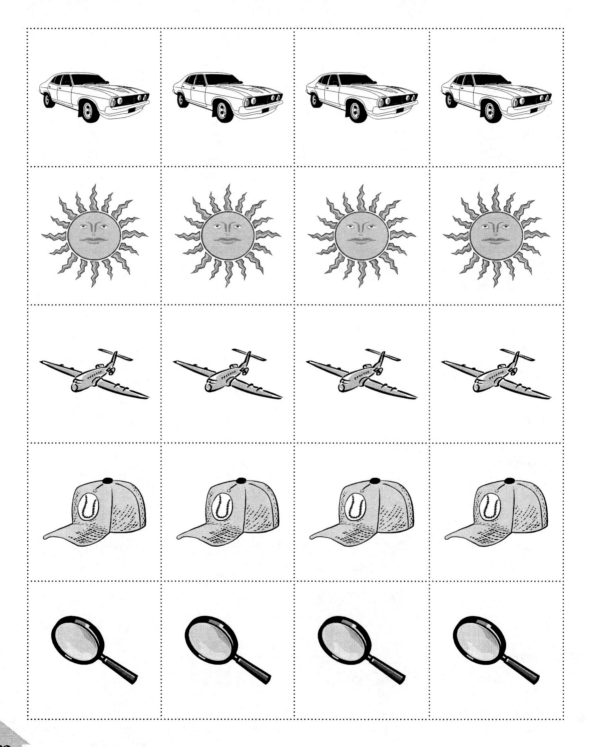

Developing Preoperational Classification and Sorting Skills: Object Classification Assessment

Instructions: Cover all rows except the one being tested. Instruct the student to point to the object that is different in the row.

Developing Preoperational Classification and Sorting Skills: Data Recording Sheet

Student: _____   Grade: _____

Teacher: _____   Date begun:_____

Date ended:_____

Date	Number of sets attempted	Number of sets classified correctly	Number of sets classified incorrectly

Notes:

204

Chapter 4 • *Tactics for Boosting Academic Achievement*   Developing Preoperational Classification and Sorting Skills

Representing Numbers 0–9 With Concrete Objects

Objective: This tactic is designed to improve number recognition (0–9).

Materials: Daily folder, Worksheet, Assessment Sheet, beans, popsicle sticks, glue, timer, and Data Recording Sheet.

Preparation: Make copies of tactic reproducibles and gather remaining tactic materials.

> Requires approximately **15 minutes** each day (two to three days per week).

Rules for using a coach: Explain the roles of the coach and the student. Assign each student a role to begin the tactic. Students should begin the tactic at the top left box of the Worksheet and work across. Explain to students that they should switch roles when they encounter a smiley face on the Worksheet. Glue ten beans to each popsicle stick to represent each unit of 10.

Coach Card

- ❑ Get materials. Go to an assigned work area. Find the day's Worksheet.
- ❑ **Coach**: Pointing to the number in the top left box, ask, "What number?"
- ❑ **Student**: Say the number.
- ❑ **Coach**: Check for accuracy and encourage the reader.
- ❑ **Coach**: Say, "Now, *show* how many."
- ❑ **Student**: Use the bean counter to show the number.
- ❑ **Coach**: Check for accuracy and encourage the reader.
- ❑ Repeat the process for each number on the Worksheet, switching the roles of coach and student each time a smiley face is encountered.
- ❑ **Assessment**: Set the timer for two minutes. Give the student an Assessment Sheet and, following the directions on the sheet, have the student complete as many numbers as possible without assistance during the two-minute period. When the timer buzzes, ask the student to stop.
- ❑ **Coach**: Record results on the Data Recording Sheet.

205

Representing Numbers 0–9 With Concrete Objects: Worksheet

Student: _____ Grade: _____

Teacher: _____ Date: _____

Instructions: The coach points to each number and asks the student to say the number and show the number using a bean counter. For each number answered correctly, the coach places a (+) in the box beside the number. Switch roles each time a smiley face (☺) is encountered.

---

5 ☐   0 ☐   9 ☐ ☺ 2 ☐

---

1 ☐   4 ☐ ☺ 5 ☐   3 ☐

---

6 ☐   1 ☐   7 ☐ ☺ 2 ☐

---

0 ☐   3 ☐ ☺ 8 ☐   1 ☐

---

9 ☐ ☺ 4 ☐   7 ☐   8 ☐

Representing Numbers 0–9 With Concrete Objects: Assessment Sheet

Student: _____   Grade: _____

Teacher: _____   Date: _____

Instructions: As the teacher points to each number, say and show the number on the bean counter. For each number answered correctly, the teacher should place a (+) in the box beside the number.

---

2 ☐   5 ☐   7 ☐   1 ☐

---

6 ☐   8 ☐   3 ☐   9 ☐

---

1 ☐   7 ☐   4 ☐   2 ☐

---

0 ☐   3 ☐   8 ☐   7 ☐

---

9 ☐   4 ☐   1 ☐   0 ☐

Representing Numbers 0–9 With Concrete Objects:
Data Recording Sheet

Student: _____ Grade: _____

Teacher: _____ Date: _____

Assessment numbers 0–9	Numbers recognized correctly (+)	Numbers represented correctly using bean counter (+)

Notes:

Representing Numbers 10–19 With Concrete Objects

Objective: This tactic is designed to improve number recognition (10–19).

Materials: Daily folder, beans, popsicle sticks, glue, Worksheet, Assessment Sheet, timer, and Data Recording Sheet.

Requires approximately **15 minutes** each day (two to three days per week).

Preparation: Make copies of tactic reproducibles and gather remaining tactic materials.

Rules for using a coach: Explain the roles of the coach and the reader. Assign each student a role to begin the tactic. Students should begin the tactic at the top left box of the Worksheet and work across. Explain to students that they should switch roles when they encounter a smiley face on the Worksheet. Glue ten beans to each popsicle stick to represent each unit of 10.

Coach Card

- ❑ Get materials. Go to an assigned work area. Find the day's Worksheet.
- ❑ **Coach**: Pointing to the number next to the top left box, ask, "What number?"
- ❑ **Student**: Say the number.
- ❑ **Coach**: Check for accuracy and encourage the reader.
- ❑ **Coach**: Say, "Now, *show* how many."
- ❑ **Student**: Use the bean counters to show the number.
- ❑ **Coach**: Check for accuracy and encourage the reader.
- ❑ Repeat the process for each number on the Worksheet, switching the roles of coach and student each time a smiley face is encountered.
- ❑ **Assessment**: Set the timer for two minutes. Give the student an Assessment Sheet and, following the directions on the sheet, have the student complete as many numbers as possible without assistance during the two-minute period. When the timer buzzes, ask the student to stop.
- ❑ **Coach**: Record results on the Data Recording Sheet.

Representing Numbers 10–19 With Concrete Objects: Worksheet

Student: _____   Grade: _____

Teacher: _____   Date: _____

Instructions: The coach points to each number and asks the student to say the number and show the number using bean counters. For each number answered correctly, the coach places a (+) in the box beside the number. Switch roles each time a smiley face (☺) is encountered.

---

15 ☐   10 ☐   19 ☐   12 ☐

---

11 ☐   14 ☐   15 ☐ ☺ 13 ☐

---

16 ☐   11 ☐ ☺ 17 ☐   12 ☐

---

10 ☐   13 ☐   18 ☐ ☺ 11 ☐

---

19 ☐   14 ☐ ☺ 17 ☐   18 ☐

Representing Numbers 10–19 With Concrete Objects: Assessment Sheet

Student: _____ Grade: _____

Teacher: _____ Date: _____

Instructions: As the teacher points to each number, say and show the number on the bean counters. For each number answered correctly, the teacher should place a (+) in the box beside the number.

10 ☐   19 ☐   11 ☐   16 ☐

12 ☐   13 ☐   15 ☐   18 ☐

11 ☐   16 ☐   10 ☐   14 ☐

17 ☐   13 ☐   18 ☐   11 ☐

19 ☐   12 ☐   17 ☐   18 ☐

Representing Numbers 10–19 With Concrete Objects: Data Recording Sheet

Student: _____   Grade: _____

Teacher: _____   Date: _____

Assessment numbers 10–19	Numbers recognized correctly (+)	Numbers represented correctly using bean counter (+)

Notes:

Representing Numbers 20–29 With Concrete Objects

Objective: This tactic is designed to improve number recognition (20–29).

Materials: Daily folder, Worksheet, Assessment Sheet, popsicle sticks, beans, glue, timer, and Data Recording Sheet.

Preparation: Make copies of tactic reproducibles and gather remaining tactic materials.

Requires approximately **15 minutes** each day (one to two times per week).

Rules for using a coach: Explain the roles of the coach and the reader. Assign each student a role to begin the tactic. Students should begin the tactic at the top left box of the Worksheet and work across. Explain to students that they should switch roles when they encounter a smiley face on the Worksheet. Glue ten beans to each popsicle stick to represent each unit of 10.

Coach Card

- ❏ Get materials. Go to an assigned work area. Find the day's Worksheet.
- ❏ **Coach**: Pointing to the number next to the top left box, ask, "What number?"
- ❏ **Student**: Say the number.
- ❏ **Coach**: Check for accuracy and encourage the reader.
- ❏ **Coach**: Say, "Now, *show* how many."
- ❏ **Student**: Use the bean counters to show the number.
- ❏ **Coach**: Check for accuracy and encourage the reader.
- ❏ Repeat the process for each number on the Worksheet, switching the roles of coach and student each time a smiley face is encountered.
- ❏ **Assessment**: Set the timer for two minutes. Give the student an Assessment Sheet and, following the directions on the sheet, have the student complete as many numbers as possible without assistance during the two-minute period. When the timer buzzes, ask the student to stop.
- ❏ **Coach**: Record the results on the Data Recording Sheet.

Representing Numbers 20–29
With Concrete Objects: Worksheet

Student: _____   Grade: _____

Teacher: _____   Date: _____

Instructions: The coach points to each number and asks the student to say the number and show the number using bean counters. For each number answered correctly, the coach places a (+) in the box beside the number. Switch roles each time a smiley face (☺) is encountered.

---

25 ☐   20 ☐ ☺ 29 ☐   22 ☐

---

21 ☐   24 ☐ ☺ 25 ☐   23 ☐

---

26 ☐   21 ☐   27 ☐ ☺ 22 ☐

---

20 ☐   23 ☐ ☺ 28 ☐   21 ☐

---

29 ☐ ☺ 24 ☐   27 ☐   28 ☐

Representing Numbers 20–29
With Concrete Objects: Assessment Sheet

Student: _____ Grade: _____

Teacher: _____ Date: _____

Instructions: As the teacher points to each number, say and show the number using bean counters. For each number answered correctly, the teacher should place a (+) in the box beside the number.

29 ☐   26 ☐   20 ☐   22 ☐

21 ☐   24 ☐   23 ☐   25 ☐

28 ☐   27 ☐   22 ☐   29 ☐

20 ☐   23 ☐   28 ☐   21 ☐

29 ☐   24 ☐   27 ☐   22 ☐

Representing Numbers 20–29
With Concrete Objects: Data Recording Sheet

Student: _____ Grade: _____

Teacher: _____ Date: _____

Assessment numbers 20–29	Numbers recognized correctly (+)	Numbers represented correctly using bean counter (+)

Notes:

Improving Number Recognition (0–9)

Objective: This tactic is designed to improve number recognition (0–9).

Materials: Daily folder, Worksheet, Assessment Sheet, timer, and Data Recording Sheet.

Preparation: Make copies of tactic reproducibles and gather remaining tactic materials.

Rules for using a coach: Explain the roles of the coach and the reader. Assign each student a role to begin the tactic. Students should begin the tactic at the top left box of the Worksheet and work across. Explain to students that they should switch roles when they encounter a smiley face on the Worksheet.

> Requires approximately **15 minutes** each day (two to three days per week).

Coach Card

❑ Get materials. Go to an assigned work area. Find the day's Worksheet.

❑ **Coach**: Pointing to the number next to the top left box, ask, "What number?"

❑ **Student**: Say the number.

❑ **Coach**: Check for accuracy and encourage the reader.

❑ **Coach**: Say, "Now, *show* how many."

❑ **Student**: Hold up your fingers to show the number.

❑ **Coach**: Check for accuracy and encourage the reader.

❑ Repeat the process for each number on the Worksheet, switching the roles of coach and student each time a smiley face is encountered.

❑ **Assessment**: Set the timer for two minutes. Give the student an Assessment Sheet and, following the directions on the sheet, have the student complete as many numbers as possible during the two-minute period. When the timer rings, ask the student to stop.

❑ **Coach**: Record results on the Data Recording Sheet.

Improving Number Recognition (0–9):
Worksheet

Student: _____ Grade: _____

Teacher: _____ Date: _____

Instructions: The coach points to each number and asks the student to say the number and show the number using bean counters. For each number answered correctly, the coach places a (+) in the box beside the number. Switch roles each time a smiley face (☺) is encountered.

---

5 ☐   0 ☐   9 ☐ ☺ 2 ☐

---

1 ☐   4 ☐ ☺ 5 ☐   3 ☐

---

6 ☐   1 ☐   7 ☐ ☺ 2 ☐

---

0 ☐   3 ☐   8 ☐   1 ☐

---

9 ☐ ☺ 4 ☐   7 ☐   8 ☐

Improving Number Recognition (0–9): Assessment Sheet

Student: _____ Grade: _____

Teacher: _____ Date: _____

Instructions: As the teacher points to each number, say and show the number using your fingers. The teacher should place a (+) in the box next to each number answered correctly.

9 ☐	10 ☐	2 ☐	8 ☐
1 ☐	9 ☐	5 ☐	7 ☐
3 ☐	6 ☐	4 ☐	0 ☐
5 ☐	9 ☐	1 ☐	3 ☐
7 ☐	8 ☐	3 ☐	2 ☐
0 ☐	6 ☐	2 ☐	8 ☐
9 ☐	7 ☐	5 ☐	1 ☐
2 ☐	5 ☐	3 ☐	9 ☐
3 ☐	8 ☐	0 ☐	6 ☐
5 ☐	1 ☐	2 ☐	8 ☐
9 ☐	4 ☐	0 ☐	5 ☐

Improving Number Recognition (0–9):
Data Recording Sheet

Student: _____   Grade: _____

Teacher: _____   Date: _____

Assessment numbers 0–9	Numbers recognized correctly (+)	Numbers represented correctly using fingers (+)

Notes:

Improving Number Recognition (10–19)

Objective: This tactic is designed to improve number recognition (10–19).

Materials: Daily folder, Worksheet, Assessment Sheet, timer, and Data Recording Sheet.

Preparation: Make copies of tactic reproducibles and gather remaining tactic materials.

Rules for using a coach: Explain the roles of the coach and the student. Assign each student a role to begin the tactic. Students should begin the tactic at the top left box of the Worksheet and work across. Explain to students they should switch roles when they encounter a smiley face on the Worksheet.

> Requires approximately **15 minutes** each day (two to three days per week).

Coach Card

- ❑ Get materials. Go to an assigned work area. Find the day's Worksheet.
- ❑ **Coach**: Pointing to the number next to the top left box, ask, "What number?"
- ❑ **Student**: Say the number.
- ❑ **Coach**: Check for accuracy and encourage the reader.
- ❑ **Coach**: Say, "Now, *show* how many."
- ❑ **Student**: Hold up your fingers to show the number.
- ❑ **Coach**: Check for accuracy and encourage the reader.
- ❑ Repeat the process for each number on the Worksheet, switching the roles of coach and student each time a smiley face is encountered.
- ❑ **Assessment**: Set the timer for two minutes. Give the student an Assessment Sheet and, following the directions on the sheet, have student complete as many numbers as possible during the two-minute period. When the timer rings, ask the student to stop.
- ❑ **Coach**: Record results on the Data Recording Sheet.

Improving Number Recognition (10–19): Worksheet

Student: _____   Grade: _____

Teacher: _____   Date: _____

Instructions: The coach points to each number and asks the student to say and show the number on his/her fingers. For each number answered correctly, the coach places a (+) in the box beside the number. Switch roles each time a smiley face (☺) is encountered.

15 ☐   10 ☐   19 ☐ ☺ 12 ☐

11 ☐   14 ☐ ☺ 15 ☐   13 ☐

16 ☐   11 ☐   17 ☐ ☺ 12 ☐

10 ☐   13 ☐   18 ☐   11 ☐

19 ☐ ☺ 14 ☐   17 ☐   18 ☐

Improving Number Recognition (10–19):
Assessment Sheet

Student: _____   Grade: _____

Teacher: _____   Date: _____

Instructions: As the teacher points to each number, say and show the number using your fingers. The teacher should place a (+) in the box next to each number answered correctly.

19 ☐	10 ☐	12 ☐	18 ☐
11 ☐	19 ☐	15 ☐	17 ☐
13 ☐	16 ☐	14 ☐	10 ☐
15 ☐	19 ☐	11 ☐	13 ☐
17 ☐	18 ☐	13 ☐	12 ☐
10 ☐	16 ☐	12 ☐	18 ☐
19 ☐	17 ☐	15 ☐	11 ☐
12 ☐	15 ☐	13 ☐	19 ☐
13 ☐	18 ☐	10 ☐	16 ☐
15 ☐	11 ☐	12 ☐	18 ☐
19 ☐	14 ☐	11 ☐	15 ☐

Tactics for Boosting Academic Achievement • Chapter 4

Improving Number Recognition (10–19):
Data Recording Sheet

Student: _____   Grade: _____

Teacher: _____   Date: _____

Assessment numbers 10–19	Numbers recognized correctly (+)	Numbers represented correctly using fingers (+)

Notes:

Improving Number Recognition (20–29)

Objective: This tactic is designed to improve number recognition (20–29).

Materials: Daily folder, Worksheet, Assessment Sheet, timer, and Data Recording Sheet.

Preparation: Make copies of tactic reproducibles and gather remaining tactic materials.

Rules for using a coach: Explain the roles of the coach and the reader. Assign each student a role to begin the tactic. Students should begin the tactic at the top left box of the Worksheet and work across. Explain to students they should switch roles when they encounter a smiley face on the Worksheet.

> Requires approximately **15 minutes** each day (two to three times per week).

Coach Card

- ❑ Get materials. Go to an assigned work area. Find the day's Worksheet.
- ❑ **Coach**: Pointing to the number next to the top left box, ask, "What number?"
- ❑ **Student**: Say the number.
- ❑ **Coach**: Check for accuracy and encourage the reader.
- ❑ **Coach**: Say, "Now, *show* how many."
- ❑ **Student**: Hold up your fingers to show the number.
- ❑ **Coach**: Check for accuracy and encourage the reader.
- ❑ Repeat the process until for each number on the Worksheet, switching the roles of coach and student each time a smiley face is encountered.
- ❑ **Assessment**: Set the timer for two minutes. Give the student an Assessment Sheet and, following the directions on the sheet, have the student complete as many numbers as possible without assistance for the two-minute period. When the timer buzzes, ask the student to stop.
- ❑ **Coach**: Record results on the Data Recording Sheet.

Improving Number Recognition (20–29): Worksheet

Student: _____ Grade: _____

Teacher: _____ Date: _____

Instructions: The coach points to each number and asks the student to say and show the number on his/her fingers. For each number answered correctly, the coach places a (+) in the box beside the number. Switch roles each time a smiley face (☺) is encountered.

25 ☐   20 ☐   29 ☐ ☺ 22 ☐

21 ☐   24 ☐ ☺ 25 ☐   23 ☐

26 ☐   21 ☐   27 ☐ ☺ 22 ☐

20 ☐   23 ☐ ☺ 28 ☐   21 ☐

29 ☐ ☺ 24 ☐   27 ☐   28 ☐

Improving Number Recognition (20–29):
Assessment Sheet

Student: _____ Grade: _____

Teacher: _____ Date: _____

Instructions: As the teacher points to each number, say and show the number on your fingers. The teacher should place a (+) in the box next to each number answered correctly.

---

29 ☐   20 ☐   25 ☐   22 ☐

---

27 ☐   25 ☐   24 ☐   21 ☐

---

26 ☐   23 ☐   27 ☐   22 ☐

---

20 ☐   25 ☐   28 ☐   21 ☐

---

29 ☐   24 ☐   27 ☐   28 ☐

Improving Number Recognition (20–29):
Data Recording Sheet

Student: _____   Grade: _____

Teacher: _____   Date: _____

Assessment numbers 20–29	Numbers recognized correctly (+)	Numbers represented correctly using fingers (+)

Notes:

Improving Number Recognition and Memorization

Objective: This tactic is designed to improve number recognition and enhance the memorization of phone numbers.

 Requires approximately **15 minutes** each day (two to three days per week).

Materials: Daily folder, phone number worksheet (student created), markers, pencil, paper, scissors, glue, timer, and Data Recording Sheet.

Preparation: Make copies of tactic reproducibles and gather remaining tactic materials. Have the student use markers to write his/her phone number on a sheet of paper (allow the student to copy the number if necessary), and make eight copies of the student's phone number sheet. Cut seven copies into individual number pieces for use during the assessment step.

Coach Card

- ❑ Get materials. Go to an assigned work area. Find the worksheet showing your phone number and a blank sheet of paper.

- ❑ Write your name, the teacher's name, your grade, and the date on the blank sheet of paper.

- ❑ Cut the numbers on the worksheet apart so that each number is on a separate paper cut out.

- ❑ Mix up the cut out numbers.

- ❑ Arrange the mixed-up number cut outs in your phone number order. Glue them in order onto the blank sheet of paper. Check your work.

- ❑ **Assessment**: Set the timer for two minutes. Mix up the seven sets of cut out numbers. Have the student arrange as many numbers in order as possible during the two-minute period. When the timer buzzes, ask the student to stop.

- ❑ **Coach**: Record results on the Data Recording Sheet.

Improving Number Recognition and Memorization: Data Recording Sheet

Student: _____   Grade: _____

Teacher: _____   Date begun: _____

                                                         Date ended: _____

Date	Total sets of numbers arranged correctly	Percent of number sets arranged correctly

Notes:

Sequencing Numbers 1–20

Objective: This tactic is designed to increase the student's ability to sequence numbers (1–20).

Materials: Daily folder, Number Squares Sheet, scissors, pencil, timer, and Data Recording Sheet.

Preparation: Make copies of tactic reproducibles and gather remaining tactic materials.

 Requires approximately **15 minutes** each day (two to three days per week).

Coach Card

❑ Get materials. Go to an assigned work area. Find the Number Squares Sheet. Cut out the number squares and arrange them out of order on a table.

❑ **Model**: Place the numbers in a row in order from 1 to 20. Count the order aloud, starting again with 1, several times before completing the row. Repeat this procedure two times.

❑ **Guided practice**: Place the number squares out of order on the table and instruct the student to put them in order from 1 to 20. (If the student waits ten seconds without placing a number or places the wrong number, show the student the correct number placement.)

❑ Instruct the student to say the number order as the sequence is being completed. Repeat this procedure two times.

❑ **Assessment**: Set the timer for two minutes. Place the number squares, out of order, in front of the student and instruct him/her to place the numbers in order from 1 to 20. Repeat this procedure up to four times during the two-minute period. When the timer rings, ask the student to stop.

❑ **Coach**: Record results on the Data Recording Sheet.

Sequencing Numbers 1–20: Number Squares Sheet

Instructions: Cut the numbers into individual squares.

1	2	3	4
5	6	7	8
9	10	11	12
13	14	15	16
17	18	19	20

Sequencing Numbers 1–20: Data Recording Sheet

Student: _____   Grade: _____

Teacher: _____   Date begun:_____

Date ended:_____

Date	Number of sets sequenced correctly	Number of sets sequenced incorrectly	Number of sets attempted

Notes:

Writing Numbers 1–10

Objective: This tactic is designed to increase the student's ability to accurately form the numbers 1 through 10 from memory.

Materials: Daily folder, Numbers Chart, Practice Worksheet, blank ruled paper, pencil, timer, and Data Recording Sheet.

Preparation: Make copies of tactic reproducibles and gather remaining tactic materials.

 Requires approximately **10 minutes** each day (one to two days per week).

Coach Card

- ☐ Get materials.

- ☐ **Model**: Referring to the Numbers Chart, trace each number with your finger twice while saying the number aloud.

- ☐ Take out the Practice Worksheet. Trace each number with a pencil twice while saying the number aloud. Practice writing each number two times showing the starting and ending points of each number.

- ☐ Give the student a blank piece of ruled paper. Instruct the student to call out a number from 1 through 10 and write the number on the line. Have the student do this for all the numbers from 1 through 10.

- ☐ **Guided practice**: Instruct the student to trace each number on the Numbers Chart with his/her finger while saying the number aloud.

- ☐ Instruct the student to trace each number on the Practice Worksheet with a pencil while saying the number aloud. Remind the student where the starting and ending points are for writing each number. Instruct the student to complete the worksheet by writing each number two times.

- ☐ **Assessment**: Give the student a piece of blank ruled paper. Set the timer for two minutes. Call out each number from 1 through 10. Instruct the student to write the numbers on the lines as they are called out. When the timer rings, ask the student to stop.

- ☐ **Coach**: Record results on the Data Recording Sheet.

Writing Numbers 1–10: Numbers Chart

1   2   3

4   5   6

7   8   9

10

Writing Numbers 1–10: Practice Worksheet

Student: _____   Grade: _____

Teacher: _____   Date: _____

1   _____   _____

2   _____   _____

3   _____   _____

4   _____   _____

5   _____   _____

6 _____   _____

7 _____   _____

8 _____   _____

9 _____   _____

10 _____   _____

Writing Numbers 1–10: Data Recording Sheet

Student: _____   Grade: _____

Teacher: _____   Date begun: _____

Date ended: _____

Date	Total numbers written correctly	Total numbers written incorrectly	Total numbers attempted

Notes:

Building Fact Fluency

Objective: This tactic is designed to build math fact fluency and increase accuracy. This tactic can be used for addition, subtraction, multiplication, or division facts.

Materials: Daily folder, math probes and corresponding answer keys (i.e., the Math Problems Worksheets for addition, subtraction, multiplication, and division), timer, pencil, and Data Recording Sheet.

 Requires approximately **7 minutes** each day (two to three times per week).

Preparation: Teach the math skill to the student prior to implementation of tactic. Make copies of tactic reproducibles (make two copies of the day's Math Problems Worksheet, completing one for use as an answer key) and gather remaining tactic materials. Teachers may choose to use free worksheets that can be found online (see list of Web sites at the end of this chapter). Prepare the Math Problems Worksheet by drawing a practice line under the first two or three rows of problems. Review students' progress and change materials weekly. Prepare a treasure chest full of items the student can earn if he/she beats his/her score from the day before. Tell student, "If you beat your score from the last math probe, which is ____, you may pick something out of the treasure chest."

Coach Card

- ❑ Get materials. Go to an assigned work area. Write names, grade, and date on the day's Math Problems Worksheet (addition, subtraction, multiplication, or division).

- ❑ Work all the problems on the rows above the practice line drawn on the worksheet with help from your teacher or coach. Check the answers together.

- ❑ **Assessment**: Set the timer for two minutes. Cover the practice problems above the practice line. Have the student work as many problems below the practice line as possible for the two-minute period. When the timer buzzes, ask the student to stop.

- ❑ Score your paper using the answer key.

- ❑ Count the number of problems you got right. Write the correct answer for the problems you missed.

- ❑ Write your score at the top of Math Problems Worksheet.

- ❑ **Coach**: Record results on the Data Recording Sheet. If the student scores higher than his/her last math probe, the student may choose a reward from the treasure chest.

Building Fact Fluency:
Math Problems Worksheet (Addition)

Student: _____   Grade: _____

Teacher: _____   Date: _____

Instructions: Find the sum for each addition problem.

$$
\begin{array}{r} 6 \\ + 7 \\ \hline \end{array}
\qquad
\begin{array}{r} 6 \\ + 3 \\ \hline \end{array}
\qquad
\begin{array}{r} 6 \\ + 2 \\ \hline \end{array}
\qquad
\begin{array}{r} 2 \\ + 10 \\ \hline \end{array}
$$

$$
\begin{array}{r} 8 \\ + 3 \\ \hline \end{array}
\qquad
\begin{array}{r} 5 \\ + 2 \\ \hline \end{array}
\qquad
\begin{array}{r} 8 \\ + 1 \\ \hline \end{array}
\qquad
\begin{array}{r} 10 \\ + 5 \\ \hline \end{array}
$$

$$
\begin{array}{r} 0 \\ + 0 \\ \hline \end{array}
\qquad
\begin{array}{r} 8 \\ + 10 \\ \hline \end{array}
\qquad
\begin{array}{r} 9 \\ + 4 \\ \hline \end{array}
\qquad
\begin{array}{r} 2 \\ + 1 \\ \hline \end{array}
$$

$$
\begin{array}{r} 7 \\ + 0 \\ \hline \end{array}
\qquad
\begin{array}{r} 5 \\ + 1 \\ \hline \end{array}
\qquad
\begin{array}{r} 3 \\ + 1 \\ \hline \end{array}
\qquad
\begin{array}{r} 4 \\ + 10 \\ \hline \end{array}
$$

$$
\begin{array}{r} 10 \\ + 8 \\ \hline \end{array}
\qquad
\begin{array}{r} 9 \\ + 2 \\ \hline \end{array}
\qquad
\begin{array}{r} 4 \\ + 7 \\ \hline \end{array}
\qquad
\begin{array}{r} 4 \\ + 1 \\ \hline \end{array}
$$

Building Fact Fluency:
Math Problems Worksheet (Subtraction)

Student: _____   Grade: _____

Teacher: _____   Date: _____

Instructions: Find the difference for each subtraction problem.

$$
\begin{array}{r} 15 \\ -\ 8 \\ \hline \end{array}
\qquad
\begin{array}{r} 9 \\ -\ 6 \\ \hline \end{array}
\qquad
\begin{array}{r} 9 \\ -\ 3 \\ \hline \end{array}
\qquad
\begin{array}{r} 8 \\ -\ 6 \\ \hline \end{array}
$$

$$
\begin{array}{r} 4 \\ -\ 0 \\ \hline \end{array}
\qquad
\begin{array}{r} 16 \\ -\ 7 \\ \hline \end{array}
\qquad
\begin{array}{r} 4 \\ -\ 2 \\ \hline \end{array}
\qquad
\begin{array}{r} 11 \\ -\ 5 \\ \hline \end{array}
$$

$$
\begin{array}{r} 19 \\ -\ 10 \\ \hline \end{array}
\qquad
\begin{array}{r} 7 \\ -\ 5 \\ \hline \end{array}
\qquad
\begin{array}{r} 6 \\ -\ 5 \\ \hline \end{array}
\qquad
\begin{array}{r} 13 \\ -\ 10 \\ \hline \end{array}
$$

$$
\begin{array}{r} 6 \\ -\ 0 \\ \hline \end{array}
\qquad
\begin{array}{r} 7 \\ -\ 4 \\ \hline \end{array}
\qquad
\begin{array}{r} 5 \\ -\ 2 \\ \hline \end{array}
\qquad
\begin{array}{r} 11 \\ -\ 2 \\ \hline \end{array}
$$

$$
\begin{array}{r} 9 \\ -\ 9 \\ \hline \end{array}
\qquad
\begin{array}{r} 10 \\ -\ 5 \\ \hline \end{array}
\qquad
\begin{array}{r} 3 \\ -\ 0 \\ \hline \end{array}
\qquad
\begin{array}{r} 7 \\ -\ 6 \\ \hline \end{array}
$$

Building Fact Fluency:
Math Problems Worksheet (Multiplication)

Student: _____   Grade: _____

Teacher: _____   Date: _____

Instructions: Find the product for each multiplication problem.

$$\begin{array}{r} 5 \\ \times\ 0 \\ \hline \end{array} \qquad \begin{array}{r} 2 \\ \times\ 6 \\ \hline \end{array} \qquad \begin{array}{r} 0 \\ \times\ 2 \\ \hline \end{array} \qquad \begin{array}{r} 5 \\ \times\ 8 \\ \hline \end{array}$$

$$\begin{array}{r} 4 \\ \times\ 7 \\ \hline \end{array} \qquad \begin{array}{r} 8 \\ \times\ 1 \\ \hline \end{array} \qquad \begin{array}{r} 9 \\ \times\ 6 \\ \hline \end{array} \qquad \begin{array}{r} 4 \\ \times\ 6 \\ \hline \end{array}$$

$$\begin{array}{r} 10 \\ \times\ 8 \\ \hline \end{array} \qquad \begin{array}{r} 3 \\ \times\ 5 \\ \hline \end{array} \qquad \begin{array}{r} 1 \\ \times\ 9 \\ \hline \end{array} \qquad \begin{array}{r} 3 \\ \times\ 4 \\ \hline \end{array}$$

$$\begin{array}{r} 6 \\ \times\ 1 \\ \hline \end{array} \qquad \begin{array}{r} 0 \\ \times\ 6 \\ \hline \end{array} \qquad \begin{array}{r} 6 \\ \times\ 5 \\ \hline \end{array} \qquad \begin{array}{r} 0 \\ \times\ 0 \\ \hline \end{array}$$

$$\begin{array}{r} 7 \\ \times\ 3 \\ \hline \end{array} \qquad \begin{array}{r} 1 \\ \times\ 7 \\ \hline \end{array} \qquad \begin{array}{r} 7 \\ \times\ 0 \\ \hline \end{array} \qquad \begin{array}{r} 0 \\ \times\ 5 \\ \hline \end{array}$$

Building Fact Fluency:
Math Problems Worksheet (Division)

Student: _____ Grade: _____

Teacher: _____ Date: _____

Instructions: Find the quotient for each division problem.

$2\overline{)4}$ $\qquad$ $3\overline{)9}$ $\qquad$ $5\overline{)10}$

$4\overline{)12}$ $\qquad$ $8\overline{)16}$ $\qquad$ $9\overline{)27}$

$1\overline{)6}$ $\qquad$ $5\overline{)25}$ $\qquad$ $2\overline{)10}$

$6\overline{)32}$ $\qquad$ $1\overline{)9}$ $\qquad$ $3\overline{)15}$

$4\overline{)20}$ $\qquad$ $3\overline{)12}$ $\qquad$ $8\overline{)24}$

Building Fact Fluency: Data Recording Sheet

Student: _____ Grade: _____

Teacher: _____ Date begun: _____

Date ended: _____

Date	Number of problems on worksheet	Number of problems answered correctly	Last score beaten? (circle one)	
			Yes	No
			Yes	No
			Yes	No
			Yes	No
			Yes	No
			Yes	No
			Yes	No
			Yes	No
			Yes	No
			Yes	No

Notes:

Building Fact Fluency—Classwide Practice

Objective: This tactic is designed to build math fact fluency and increase accuracy. This tactic can be used for addition, subtraction, multiplication, or division facts.

> Requires approximately **10 minutes** each day (two to three times per week).

Materials: Daily folder, index cards to make flash card sets, markers, teacher-created or Web site math probe worksheets (i.e., worksheet containing problems for the day's problem skill: addition, subtraction, multiplication, or division), timer, Performance Graph Sheet, and Worksheet Data Recording Sheet.

Preparation: Make copies of tactic reproducibles and gather remaining tactic materials. For the problem skill being taught, make one set of flash cards for every two students using the markers and index cards (write the problem on one side and the answer on the lower corner of the opposite side), and make copies of selected math probe worksheets. See list at the end of this chapter of suggested Web sites offering free worksheets.

Coach Card

- ☐ Get materials. As you pass out the day's flash cards, instruct students to quickly and quietly find their math partners.

- ☐ Set the timer for three minutes and tell students, "Begin practicing." (Practicing is defined as one partner presenting all the flash cards to the other partner, who gives answers to the problems presented on the cards.)

- ☐ When the timer rings, tell students, "Stop. Give the flash cards to your partner."

- ☐ Again, set the timer for three minutes and tell students, "Begin practicing."

- ☐ When the timer rings, tell students, "Stop practicing."

- ☐ Pass out the day's math probe worksheets face down on paired students' work areas. Tell students, "Write your name on the back of your worksheet. Don't turn it over until I tell you to."

- ☐ **Assessment**: Set the timer for two minutes. Say, "On your mark, get set." Begin the timer, and say, "Go." When the timer rings, tell students, "Stop. Hold your papers up in the air so that I can see that you are no longer working."

- ☐ Tell students, "Trade papers with your math partner for scoring. When I call out the answers, circle the incorrect answers."

- ☐ Call out the correct answers. Review with the entire class answers that several students missed.

- ☐ Tell students, "Return papers to their owners. If you missed problems, write the correct answer under the problem your partner circled."

- ☐ Tell students, "Write the number of problems you missed at the top of your worksheet and pass your papers to the front so I can pick them up."

- ☐ **Coach**: Shuffle the worksheets then randomly draw one from the stack. If the score on this randomly selected worksheet is higher than a randomly selected score from the day before (or the class median if you have calculated it), then deliver a classwide reward (e.g., five minutes of free time). Record results on each student's Worksheet Data Recording Sheet.

- ☐ **Student**: Take out Performance Graph Sheet. Write the date on the bottom axis. Place a dot on the line that intersects the date and number correct. Connect dots.

Building Fact Fluency—Classwide Practice:
Data Recording Sheet (Worksheet)

Student: _____   Grade: _____

Teacher: _____   Date begun:_____

Date ended:_____

Date	Number of problems on worksheet	Number of problems answered correctly	Last score beaten? (circle one)	
			Yes	No
			Yes	No
			Yes	No
			Yes	No
			Yes	No
			Yes	No
			Yes	No
			Yes	No
			Yes	No
			Yes	No

Notes:

Building Fact Fluency—Classwide Practice:
Performance Graph Sheet (Assessment Component)

Student: _____   Grade: _____

Teacher: _____   Date begun:_____

Date ended:_____

10										
9										
8										
7										
6										
5										
4										
3										
2										
1										
0										

Date ____ ____ ____ ____ ____ ____ ____ ____ ____ ____

Building Multiplication Fact Fluency

Objective: This tactic is designed to build fluency with multiplication facts while simultaneously decreasing errors.

Materials: Daily folder, index cards to make flash cards of multiplication facts, multiplication problems worksheet (teacher-created or from a Web site), timer, Performance Graph Sheet, Worksheet Data Recording Sheet.

 Requires approximately **5 minutes** each day (two to three times per week).

Preparation: Make copies of tactic reproducibles and gather remaining tactic materials. For multiplication facts being taught (e.g., multiplication of 3s), make flash cards using the index cards and markers, and construct a multiplication problems worksheet (and corresponding answer key) with the same facts randomly arranged. See list at the end of this chapter of suggested Web sites offering free worksheets.

Coach Card

❑ Gather materials. Go to an assigned work area.

❑ Find the day's multiplication flash cards and present each flash card to the student while verbally prompting the student to answer the problem (e.g., "What is 3×3?").

❑ Praise correct responses that occur within three seconds of the prompt ("That's right, 3×3 is 9").

❑ If no response occurs within three seconds or the student gives an incorrect response, give the student the answer ("3×3 is 9"), and immediately re-deliver the verbal prompt ("What is 3×3?").

❑ Present the entire set of flash cards twice.

❑ **Assessment**: Set the timer for two minutes. Give the student a multiplication problems worksheet with instructions to do the following when you say "Start": Complete as many problems as possible before the timer rings, work horizontally across the paper without skipping any problems, and put the pencil down when the timer rings.

❑ At the end of the two-minute interval, give the student the worksheet answer key, instructing him/her to circle each error and write the correct response underneath.

❑ Direct the student to calculate the number correct per timed period (two minutes) and the total number of errors made. Using a sheet of graph paper, the student may graph his/her progress across days.

❑ **Student**: Take out the Performance Graph Sheet. Write the date on the horizontal X axis. Draw a dot on the line that intersects the date and number correct. Connect the new dot to the dot from previous day.

❑ **Coach**: Record results on the Performance Graph Sheet (Assessment Component).

Building Multiplication Fact Fluency:
Data Recording Sheet (Worksheet)

Student: _____   Grade: _____

Teacher: _____   Date begun:_____

                                               Date ended:_____

Date	Set of multiplication facts assessed (1s, 2s, 3s, etc.)	Total multiplication problems answered correctly	Total multiplication problems answered incorrectly	Percent correct

Notes:

Building Multiplication Fact Fluency:
Performance Graph Sheet (Assessment Component)

Student: _____   Grade: _____

Teacher: _____   Date begun:_____

Date ended:_____

10										
9										
8										
7										
6										
5										
4										
3										
2										
1										
0										

Date   ____ ____ ____ ____ ____ ____ ____ ____ ____ ____

Building Multiplication Fact Fluency Using Self-Correction

Objective: This tactic is designed to build fluency with multiplication facts while simultaneously decreasing errors.

Materials: Daily folder, index cards to make flash cards of multiplication facts, multiplication problems worksheet and answer key (teacher-created or from Web site), timer, Performance Graph Sheet, and Worksheet Data Recording Sheet.

 Requires approximately **5 minutes** each day (two to three times per week).

Preparation: Make copies of tactic reproducibles and gather remaining tactic materials. For multiplication facts being taught (e.g., multiplication of 3s) make flash cards using the index cards and markers, and construct a multiplication problems worksheet (and corresponding answer key) with the same facts randomly arranged. See list at the end of this chapter of suggested Web sites offering free worksheets.

Coach Card

- ❑ Gather materials.
- ❑ Practice a set of multiplication flash cards with the student.
- ❑ Administer a two-minute timed test of the multiplication problems worksheet that corresponds to the flash cards.
- ❑ Have the student place the worksheet answer key next to the worksheet and compare his/her answers to the answers on the answer key.
- ❑ Have the student circle any errors on his/her worksheet, read the problem again, and write the correct answer (from the answer key) next to the incorrect answer circled.
- ❑ Have the student count the number of correct answers, then write the number correct at the top of the worksheet and circle it.
- ❑ Have the student count the number of answers circled because they were errors, then write this number at the top of the worksheet.
- ❑ **Assessment**: Set the timer for two minutes. Give the student a multiplication problems

worksheet with instructions to do the following when you say "Start": Complete as many problems as possible before the timer rings, work horizontally across the paper without skipping any problems, and put the pencil down when the timer rings.

- ❑ At the end of the two-minute interval, give the student the worksheet answer key and instruct him/her to circle each error and write the correct response underneath. Ask the student to write both the number correct and the number incorrect at the top of the Assessment Worksheet.
- ❑ The student may record the results of the Assessment Worksheet on his/her Progress Graph Sheet by finding the day of the assessment along the bottom axis of the graph, finding the number answered correctly on the side axis, and making a dot on the graph that marks both spots, and then doing the same for the number of errors.
- ❑ **Coach**: Record results on the Worksheet Data Recording Sheet.

Building Multiplication Fact Fluency Using
Self-Correction: Data Recording Sheet (Worksheet)

Student: _____   Grade: _____

Teacher: _____   Date begun:_____

Date ended:_____

Date	Set of multiplication facts assessed (1s, 2s, 3s, etc.)	Total multiplication problems answered correctly	Total multiplication problems answered incorrectly	Percent correct

Notes:

Building Fact Fluency Using Self-Correction:
Performance Graph Sheet (Assessment Component)

Student: _____ Grade: _____

Teacher: _____ Date begun: _____

Date ended: _____

10										
9										
8										
7										
6										
5										
4										
3										
2										
1										
0										

Date ____ ____ ____ ____ ____ ____ ____ ____ ____ ____

Organizing Math Word Problems Using a Checklist

Objective: This tactic is designed to increase problem-solving skills in math through the use of a checklist.

Materials: Daily folder, math word problem, Example Worksheet, Worksheet, pencil, highlighter (optional), timer, and Data Recording Sheet.

Preparation: Make copies of tactic reproducibles and gather remaining tactic materials. Construct worksheet containing math word/story problem. Attach math word problem to the worksheet. See list at the end of this chapter of suggested Web sites offering free worksheets.

 Requires approximately **15 minutes** each day (one to two times per week).

Coach Card

- ❑ Get materials. Go to an assigned work area. Find the day's math word problem, Worksheet.
- ❑ Write name, grade, and date on the Worksheet (see completed Example Worksheet).
- ❑ Read the word problem.
- ❑ Underline or highlight key words, sentences, and phrases.
- ❑ Decide what math sign to use $(+, -, \times, \div)$.
- ❑ On the Worksheet, circle the sign to be used to solve the problem.
- ❑ Set up the problem in the box on the Worksheet.
- ❑ Solve the problem on the Worksheet.
- ❑ On the Worksheet, write a sentence for the final answer.
- ❑ Score your worksheet with the teacher's help. Write the number correct at the top of the worksheet.
- ❑ **Assessment**: Set the timer for two minutes. Present the student with a word problem. Have student use the Coach Card to complete the word problem without assistance. When timer buzzes, ask the student to stop.
- ❑ **Coach**: Record results on the Data Recording Sheet.

Organizing Math Word Problems Using a Checklist: Example Worksheet

Student: _____ Grade: _____

Teacher: _____ Date: _____

Meghan collects rocks. Meghan has 20 rocks. Her friend Mashaal gave her 7 more. How many rocks does she have all together?

---

1. What sign do I use? (Circle one)   +   −   ×   ÷

2. Set up the problem in the box below.

$$
\begin{array}{ll}
20 & \text{rocks} \\
+\ \ 7 & \text{more} \\
\hline
27 & \text{rocks}
\end{array}
$$

3. Write a sentence.

   Meghan has 27 rocks. _____

   _____

   _____

   _____

   _____

Organizing Math Word Problems Using a Checklist:
Worksheet

Student: _____   Grade: _____

Teacher: _____   Date: _____

1. What sign do I use? (Circle one)   +   −   ×   ÷

2. Set up the problem in the box below.

3. Write a sentence.

_____

_____

_____

_____

_____

Organizing Math Word Problems Using a Checklist: Data Recording Sheet

Student: _____ Grade: _____

Teacher: _____ Date begun: _____

Date ended: _____

Date	Highlighted key words within problem?	Chose correct operation?	Aligned problem appropriately?	Answer correct?
_____				
_____				
_____				
_____				
_____				
_____				
_____				
_____				
_____				

Notes:

Solving Math Word Problems Using Clues and Key Words

Objective: This tactic is designed to increase problem-solving skills in math through the use of clues and key words.

Materials: Daily folder, Chart of Clues and Key Words, math word problems worksheet (teacher-created or from a Web site), pencil, timer, and Data Recording Sheet.

Preparation: Make copies of tactic reproducibles and gather remaining tactic materials. Construct worksheets containing math word/story problems. See list at the end of this chapter of suggested Web sites offering free worksheets.

 Requires approximately **15 minutes** each day (one to two times per week).

Coach Card

- ❑ Get materials. Go to an assigned work area. Find the day's math problem worksheet and the Chart of Clues and Key Words.

- ❑ Write your name and date on the worksheet.

- ❑ Read the first problem on the worksheet.

- ❑ Using the Chart, highlight key words in the problem.

- ❑ Using the Chart to help you decide what math sign(s) to use (+ , – , × , ÷).

- ❑ Set up the problem.

- ❑ Solve the problem (show all work).

- ❑ With the teacher's assistance, score your paper.

- ❑ **Assessment**: Set the timer for four minutes. Have the student read and complete a word problem, using the Chart and without teacher assistance. When the timer rings, ask the student to stop.

- ❑ **Coach**: Record results on the Data Recording Sheet.

Solving Math Word Problems Using
Clues and Key Words: Chart of Clues and Key Words

Add (+)	Subtract (–)	Multiply (×)	Divide (÷)
added to	decreased by	increased/ decreased by a factor of	divided by
combined	difference between		how many in each group
how many more	fewer than	multiple of	out of
in all	flew away	multiplied by	per
increased by	gave away	times	percent (divide by 100)
more	how many left	product of	quotient of
more than	how many more		ratio of
plus	less		
sum	less than		
together	minus		
total of	sold		

Solving Math Word Problems Using
Clues and Key Words: Data Recording Sheet

Student: _____   Grade: _____

Teacher: _____   Date begun: _____

                                                      Date ended: _____

Date	Key word(s)	Math sign(s) used?	Problem set up correctly?	Problem solved correctly?

Notes:

Web Sites Offering Free Math Worksheets

www.edhelper.com/math

This excellent Web site provides an array of pre-made mathematical worksheets ranging from simple addition to algebra. It also provides resources and materials in all curriculum areas.

http://sssoftware.com/freeworksheets

This Web site offers pre-made addition, subtraction, multiplication, and division worksheets, available in both whole-number and decimal formats. Also available are addition and subtraction worksheets with or without regrouping and division worksheets with or without remainders. A completed page of solutions is provided for each worksheet.

http://www.rhlschool.com

This Web site contains an array of curriculum materials. Pre-made math worksheets can be generated in the areas of addition, subtraction, multiplication, division, and rounding. This Web site also offers some excellent reading probes.

http://www.mathgen.com

This Web site offers pre-made math worksheets containing addition, subtraction, multiplication, division, and rounding.

http://superkids.com

This highly recommended Web site offers a vast array of worksheets for addition, subtraction, multiplication, division, fractions, comparing numbers, and rounding.

http://schooldiscovery.com/teachingtools/worksheetgenerator

This Web site provides not only a number of pre-made worksheets for addition, subtraction, and multiplication, but it also offers individual worksheet customization.

References

Adams, G. L., & Engelmann, S. (1996). *Research on direct instruction: 25 years beyond DISTAR*. Seattle, WA: Educational Achievement Systems.

Adams, M. J. (1990). *Beginning to read: Thinking and learning about print*. Cambridge, MA: MIT Press.

Albin, R. W., & Horner, R. H. (1988). Generalization with precision. In R. H. Horner, G. Dunlap, & R. L. Koegel (Eds.), *Generalization and maintenance: Lifestyle changes in applied settings* (pp. 99–120). Baltimore: Paul H. Brookes.

Arreaga-Mayer, C., Carta, J. J., & Tapia, Y. (1994). Ecobehavioral assessment of bilingual special education settings: The opportunity to respond. In R. Gardner, D. M. Sainato, J. O. Cooper, T. E. Heron, W. E. Heward, J. Eshleman, & T. A. Grossi (Eds.), *Behavior analysis in education* (pp. 225–239). Pacific Grove, CA: Brooks/Cole.

Barker, R. (1968). *Ecological psychology*. Stanford, CA: Stanford University Press.

Barker, R. (Ed.). (1963). *The stream of behavior*. New York: Appleton-Century-Crofts.

Becker, W., & Carnine, D. W. (1981). Direct instruction: A behavior theory model for comprehensive educational intervention with the disadvantaged. In S. W. Bijou & R. Ruiz (Eds.), *Behavior modification: Contributions to education* (pp. 145–210). Hillsdale, NJ: Lawrence Erlbaum Associates.

Becker, W., Engelmann, S., & Thomas, D. (1971). *Teaching: A course in applied psychology*. Chicago: SRA Associates.

Becker, W. C. (1971). Teaching concepts and operations, or how to make kids smart. In W. C. Becker, S. Engelmann, & D. Thomas (Eds.), *Teaching: A course in applied psychology* (pp. 401–423. Chicago: SRA Associates.

Bereiter, C., & Engelmann, S. (1966). *Teaching disadvantaged children in the preschool*. Engelwood Cliffs, NJ: Prentice-Hall.

Bessellieu, F. B., & Kozloff, M. A. (1999). *Direct instruction learning communities.* Unpublished manuscript, Watson School of Education, University of North Carolina at Wilmington.

Binder, C. (1996). Behavioral fluency: Evolution of a new paradigm. *Behavior Analyst, 19*, 163–197.

Binder, C. and Watkins, C. L. (1990). Precision teaching and direct instruction: Measurably superior instructional technology in schools. *Performance Improvement Quarterly, 3*, 74–95.

Binder, C., Haughton, E., & Van Eyk, D. (1990). Precision teaching attention span. *Teaching Exceptional Children, Spring*, 24–27.

Bock, G., Stebbins, L., & Proper, E. (1977). *Education as experimentation* (Vols. 4-A & 4-B). *A planned variation model. Effects of follow through models.* Washington, DC: Abt Associates.

Bronfenbrenner, U. (1979). *The ecology of human development.* Cambridge, MA: Harvard University Press.

Caltagirone, P. J., & Glover, C. E. (1985). Precision learning assessment: An alternative to traditional assessment techniques. *B. C. Journal of Special Education, 9*, 355–363.

Catania, A. C. (1998). *Learning* (4th ed.). Upper Saddle River, NJ: Prentice Hall.

Cobb, C., Wood, T., & Yackel, E. (1990). Classrooms as learning environments for teachers and researchers. In R. B. Davis, C. A. Maher, & N. Noddings (Eds.), *Constructivist views on the teaching and learning of mathematics.* Reston, VA: National Council of Teachers of Mathematics.

Connolly, K., & Dalgleish, M. (1989). The emergence of tool-using in infancy. *Developmental Psychology, 25*(6), 894–912.

Cox, A. R. (1992). *Foundations for literacy: Structures and techniques for multisensory teaching of basic written English language skills.* Cambridge, MA: Educators Publishing Service.

Darch, C., Gersten, R., & Taylor, R. (1987). Evaluation of Williamsburg County direct instruction program: Factors leading to success in rural elementary programs. *Research in Rural Education, 4*, 111–118.

Deno, S. L., Marston, D., & Mirkin, P. K. (1980). Relationships among simple measures of written expression and performance on standardized achievement tests (Research Report No. 22). Minneapolis: University of Minnesota, Institute for Research on Learning Disabilities.

Dougherty, K. M., & Johnston, J. M. (1996). Overlearning, fluency, and automaticity. *Behavior Analyst, 19*, 289–292.

Ehly, S. (1986). *Peer tutoring: A guide for school psychologists*. Washington, DC: National Association of School Psychologists.

Ellis, E. S., Worthington, L. A., & Larkin, M. J. (1994). Executive summary of the research synthesis on effective teaching principles and the design of quality tools for educators. Eugene: University of Oregon, National Center to Improve the Tools of Educators. http://idea.uoregon.edu/~ncite/

Engelmann, S. (1969). *Conceptual learning*. San Rafael, CA: Dimensions.

Engelmann, S., Carnine, D., Kelly, B., & Engelmann, O. (1996). *Connecting math concepts: Lesson sampler-for levels A, B, C, and D*. Worthington, OH: SRA/McGraw-Hill.

Engelmann, S., Osborn, J., Osborn, S., & Zoref, L. (1995). *Reading mastery 5: Presentation book B*. Columbus, OH: SRA/Macmillan/McGraw-Hill.

Finn, C. E., & Ravitch, D. (1996). Educational reform 1995–1996. *A report from the Educational Excellence Network*. http://www.edinformatics.com/reform/profdevelop.htm

Fogel, A. (1992). Movement and communication in infancy: The social dynamics of development. *Human Movement Science, 11*(4), 387–423.

Frith, U. (1990). *Unexpected spelling problems: Cognitive processes in spelling*. London: Academic Press.

Frith, U., & Frith, C. (1980). *Relationships between reading and spelling*. Baltimore: York Press.

Fuchs, L. S., & Deno, S. L. (1994). Must instructionally useful performance assessment be based in the curriculum? *Exceptional Children, 61*, 15–24.

Fuchs, L. S., Fuchs, D., Hamlett, C. L., & Ferguson, C. (1992). Effects of expert system consultation within curriculum-based measurement using a reading maze task. *Exceptional Children, 58*, 436–450.

Fuchs, L. S., Fuchs, D., Hamlett, C. L., & Stecker, P. M. (1991). Effects of curriculum-based measurement and consultation on teacher planning and student achievement in mathematics operations. *American Educational Research Journal, 28*, 617–641.

Fulk, B .M., & King, K. (2001). Classwide peer tutoring at work. *Teaching Exceptional Children, 34*, 49–53.

Fulk, B. M., & Stormont-Spurgin, M. (1995). Spelling interventions for students with disabilities: A review. *Journal of Special Education, 28*(4), 488–513.

Garcia-Vazquez, E., & Ehly, S. (1995). Best practices in facilitating peer tutoring programs. In A. Thomas & J. Grimes (Eds.), *Best Practices in School Psychology* (Vol. 3, pp. 403–411). Washington, DC: National Institute of Child Health and Human Development.

Gardner, R., Sainato, D. M., Cooper, J. O., Heron, T. E., Heward, W. L., Eshleman, J. W., & Grossi, T. A. (1994). *Behavior analysis in education.* Pacific Grove, CA: Brooks/Cole.

Gersten, R., Keating, T., & Becker, W. C. (1988). Continued impact of the direct instruction model: Longitudinal studies of follow through students. *Education and Treatment of Children, 11,* 318–327.

Gersten, R., Woodward, J., & Darch, C. (1986). Direct instruction: A research-based approach to curriculum design and teaching. *Exceptional Children, 53,* 17–31.

Gillingham, A., & Stillman, B. W. (1997). *The Gillingham manual: Remedial training for children with specific disability in reading, writing, and penmanship.* Cambridge, MA: Educators Publishing Service.

Good, R. H., Simmons, D. C., & Smith, S. B. (1998). Effective academic intervention in the United States: Evaluating and enhancing the acquisition of early reading skills. *School Psychology Review, 27*(1), 45–56.

Graham, S., & Harris, K. R. (1994). Implications of constructivism for teaching writing to students with special needs. *Journal of Special Education, 28,* 275–289.

Grossen, B. (1996). *How shall we group to achieve excellence with equity?* Eugene: University of Oregon Press.

Hamblin, R. L, Buckholdt, D., Ferritor, D., Kozloff, M., & Blackwell, L. (1971). *The humanization processes.* New York: John Wiley and Sons.

Hammill, D., & Larsen, S. (1983). *Test of written language.* Austin, TX: Pro-Ed.

Haring, N. G. (1988). *Generalization for students with severe handicaps: Strategies and solutions.* Seattle: University of Washington Press.

Haring, N. G., White, O. R. and Liberty, K. A. (1978). *An investigation of phases of learning and facilitating instructional events for the severely handicapped. An annual progress report, 1977–78.* Bureau of Education of the Handicapped, Project No. 443CH70564. Seattle: University of Washington, College of Education.

Haughton, E. C. (1980). Practicing practices: Learning by activity. *Behavior Analyst, 1,* 3–20.

Helm, D. T. (1989). Some features of verbal prompts. In D. T. Helm, W. T. Anderson, A. J. Mehan, & A. W. Rawls (Eds.), *The interaction order* (pp. 68–80). New York: Irvington Publishers.

Homans, G. C. (1961). *Social behavior: Its elementary forms.* New York: Harcourt, Brace and World.

Hunt, K. L. (1965). Grammatical structures written at three grade levels (NCTE Research Report No. 3). Urbana, IL: National Council for Teachers of English.

Hunt, K. L. (1977). Early blooming and late blooming syntactic structures. In C. Cooper and L. Odell (Eds.), *Evaluating writing* (pp. 91–104). Washington, DC: National Council of Teachers of English.

Isaacson, S. (1985). Assessing written language skills. In C. S. Simon (Ed.), Communication skills and classroom success: Assessment methodologies for language-learning disabled students (pp. 403–424). San Diego: College-Hill Press.

Johnson, K. R. and Layng, T. V. J. (1992). Breaking the structuralist barrier: Literacy and numeracy with fluency. *American Psychologist, 47,* 1475–1490.

Johnson, K. R. and Layng, T. V. J. (1996). On terms and procedures: Fluency. *Behavior Analyst, 19,* 281–288.

Jones, E. D., & Krouse, J. P. (1988). The effectiveness of data-based instruction by student teachers in classrooms for pupils with mild learning handicaps. *Teacher Education and Special Education, 11,* 9–19.

Jones, E. D., Southern, W. T., & Brigham, F. J. (1998). Curriculum-based assessment: Testing what is taught and teaching what is tested. *Intervention in School and Clinic, 33,* 239–249.

Jordon, J. B. and Robbins, L. S. (1971). *Let's try doing something else.* Arlington, VA: Council for Exceptional Children.

Kameenui, E. J., & Carnine, D. W. (1998). *Effective teaching strategies that accommodate diverse learners.* Upper Saddle River, NJ: Merrill.

Kozloff, M. (1988). *Productive interaction with students, children, and clients.* Springfield, IL: Charles C. Thomas.

Kozloff, M. A. (1994). *Improving educational outcomes for children with disabilities: Principles for assessment, program planning, and evaluation.* Baltimore: Paul H. Brookes Publisher.

Kunzelmann, H. P., Cohen, M., Hulten, W., Martin, G., & Mingo, A. (1970). *Precision teaching: An initial training sequence.* Seattle, WA: Special Child Publications.

Lee, L., & Canter, S. (1971). Developmental sentence scoring: A clinical procedure for estimating syntactic development in children's spontaneous speech. *Journal of Speech and Hearing Disorders, 36,* 315–340.

Lennox, C., & Siegel, L. S. (1996). The development of phonological rules and visual strategies in average and poor spellers. *Journal of Experimental Child Psychology, 62,* 60–83.

Lennox, C., & Siegel, L. S. (1998). Phonological and orthographic processes in good and poor spellers. In C. Hulme & R. Joshi (Eds.), *Reading and spelling development disorders.* Mahwah, NJ: Lawrence Erlbaum Associates.

Lindsley, O. R. (1990). Precision teaching: By teachers for children. *Teaching Exceptional Children, Spring,* 10–15.

Lindsley, O. R. (1991). From technical jargon to plain English for application. *Journal of Applied Behavior Analysis, 24,* 449–458.

Lindsley, O. R. (1993). Our discoveries over 28 years. *Journal of Precision Teaching, 10,* 11–13.

Lindsley, O. R. (1996). Is fluency free-operant response-response chaining? *Behavior Analyst, 19,* 211–224.

Manset, G. & Semmel, M. I. (1997). Are inclusive programs for students with mild disabilities effective? A comparative review of model programs. *Journal of Special Education, 31,* 155–180.

Marston, D., & Deno, S. L. (1981). *The reliability of simple, direct measures of written expression* (Research Report No. 50). Minneapolis: University of Minnesota, Institute for Research on Learning Disabilities.

Marston, D., Fuchs, L., & Deno, S. L. (1985). Measuring pupil progress: A comparison of standardized achievement tests and curriculum-based measures. *Diagnostique, 11,* 77–90.

McDermott, R. P. (1993). The acquisition of a child with a learning disability. In S. Chaiklin & J. Lave (Eds.), *Understanding practice: Perspectives on activity and context* (pp. 269–305). Cambridge, UK: Cambridge University Press.

Mercer, C. D., Jordan, L., & Miller, S. P. (1994). Implications of constructivism for teaching math to students with moderate to mild disabilities. *Journal of Special Education, 38,* 290–306.

Meyer, L. (1984). Long-term academic effects of the direct instruction Project Follow Through. *Elementary School Journal, 84,* 380–394.

Meyer, L., Gersten, R., & Gutkin, J. (1983). Direct instruction: A Project Follow Through success story in an inner-city school. *Elementary School Journal, 84,* 241–252.

Moats, L. C. (1995). *Spelling development, disability, and instruction.* Baltimore: York Press.

Montgomery, A. F., & Rossi, R. J. (1994). Becoming at risk of failure in America's schools. In R. J. Rossi (Ed.), *Schools and students at risk*. New York: Teachers College Press.

Mundschenk, N. A., and Sasso, G. M. (1995). Assessing sufficient social exemplars for students with autism. *Behavioral Disorders, 21,* 62–78.

Noddings, N. (1990). Constructivism in mathematics education. In R. Davis, C. Maher, & N. Noddings (Eds.), *Constructivist views on the teaching and learning of mathematics*. Reston, VA: National Council of Teachers of Mathematics.

Patterson, G. R., Reid, J. B., & Dishion, T. J. (1989). *Antisocial boys*. Eugene, OR: Cataglia.

Pierce, C. S. (1977). The fixation of belief. *Popular Science Monthly*, November, 1–15.

Plaud, J. J. and Gaither, G. A. (1996). Behavioral momentum: Implications and development from reinforcement theories. *Behavior Modification, 2,* 183–201.

Potts, L., Eshleman, J. W., & Cooper, J. O. (1993). Ogden Lindsley and the historical development of precision teaching. *Behavior Analyst, 16,* 177–189.

Schloss, P. J., & Smith, M. A. (1998). *Applied behavior analysis in the classroom*. Boston: Allyn & Bacon.

Schumm, J. S., & Vaughn, S. (1992). Planning for mainstreamed special education students: Perceptions of general classroom teachers. *Exceptionality, 3,* 81–98.

Sidman, M. (1989). *Coercion and its fallout*. Boston: Authors' Cooperative.

Skinner, B. F. (1938). *The behavior of organisms: An experimental analysis*. New York: Appleton-Century.

Skinner, B.F. (1953). *Science and human behavior*. New York: Free Press.

Stein, M., Carnine, D., & Dixon, R. (1998). Direct instruction: Integrating curriculum design and effective teaching practice. *Intervention in School and Clinic, 33,* 4, 227–335.

Summey, H. K., & Strahan, D. B. (1997). An exploratory study of mainstreamed seventh-graders' perceptions of an inclusive approach to instruction. *Remedial and Special Education, 18,* 36–45.

Teale, W., & Yokota, J. (2000). Beginning reading and writing: Perspectives on instruction. In D. S. Strickland & L. M. Morrow (Eds.), *Beginning reading and writing: Language and literacy series* (pp. 3–21). Newark, DE: International Reading Association.

Tindal, G. A., & Marston, D. B. (1990). Classroom-based assessment: Evaluating instructional outcomes. Columbus, OH: Merrill.

Ullmann, L. P., & Krasner, L. (1966). *Case studies in behavior modification.* New York: Holt, Rinehart and Winston.

Ulrich, R., Stachnick, T., & Mabry, J. (1970). *Control of human behavior* (Vol. 2): *From cure to prevention.* Glenview, IL: Scott, Foresman.

Videen, J., Deno, S. L., & Marston, D. (1982). *Correct word sequences: A valid indicator of proficiency in written expression* (Research Report No. 84). Minneapolis: University of Minnesota, Institute for Research on Learning Disabilities.

von Glasersfeld, E. (1984). An introduction to radical constructivism. In P. Watzlawick (Ed.), *The invented reality.* New York: Norton.

von Glasersfeld, E. (1995). A constructivist approach to teaching mathematics. In L. P. Stefe & J. Gale (Eds.), *Constructivism in education.* Hillsdale, NJ: Lawrence Erlbaum Associates.

Watkins, C. (1997). Project Follow Through: A case study of contingencies influencing instructional practices of the educational establishment. Cambridge, MA: Cambridge Center for Behavioral Studies.

Wesson, C. L. (1991). Curriculum-based measurement and two models of follow-up consultation, *Exceptional Children, 57,* 246–256.

White, O. R., & Haring, N. G. (1980). *Exceptional teaching.* Columbus, OH: Charles Merrill.

Wolery, M., Bailey, D. B., Jr., & Sugai, G. M. (1988). *Effective teaching: Principles and procedures of applied behavior analysis with exceptional students.* Boston: Allyn & Bacon.

Zigmond, N., & Miller, S. E. (1986). Assessment for instructional planning. *Exceptional Children, 52,* 501–509.